THREE WEEKS TO LIVE

My Journey From Then... to Now

a memoir by
Karen Owen

TREATY OAK PUBLISHERS

PUBLISHER'S NOTE

This is a work of personal inspiration. All text and images are based on the author's experiences.

Printed and published in the United States of America

TREATY OAK PUBLISHERS

ISBN-978-1-943658-97-8

DEDICATION

For my soulmate Howard,
my amazing family,
and my ever-supportive prayer warriors and friends.

You are the wind beneath my wings!

TABLE OF CONTENTS

2018

The Beginning of My Unexpected Journey
Where to begin?

Progress
Just getting started

On a Roll – and Happy Valentine's Day
Full body scan on Valentine's Day – really?

Happy Weekend
Balancing a Gyroscope

And One More Diet Tip
Broccolini, bok choy in my backyard???

It's Hard Work
harder than my full-time job at IBM

Guess I'm a 2nd Weeker...
and full-time member of the "Cancer Club"

Grateful for Better Days
still in research mode

The Most Memorable Afternoon
Damn Joy Party

Another Monday Bump in the Road
followed by a wig shop visit, not a bar?

Starving
now I'm a TX criminal, too

It Must Be Monday
from short to gone

And It Was the Longest Monday
can't always count on your GPS

Hump Day Update
remember those college days?

There's No Place Like Home
beautiful scarves will sustain

Gonna Be an Intense Week
Watson Oncology results

A Wonderful Weekend at Lizzie's Fairytale Wedding
*from a horse-drawn carriage arrival to
a fireworks departure – and everything in-between*

T.G.I.F.
no news is good news?

A New Normal
positive attitude and prayer

So Grateful for Beautiful Weather
Happy Easter

It's Saturday Already!
nupagen shots required

Triple C Day #4
6 hours, 5 bags
Who Pulled My Plug?
too much zzzzzz time

Best Bluebonnets Ever
Scott: what a son!

A 'New Normal' Week in Review
doctors, doctors, and more doctors

Good News Wednesday
laser treatments designed for SUCCESSFUL healing

Challenging Saturday
missing a special wedding

All Systems GO
wildflowers and hummingbirds

Cloudy Monday
drizzly, cloudy, overcast

Wednesday Has Burst Among Us
wearing an ankle bracelet

Trip-C Day #6
my poison cocktail

T.G.I.F.
enjoying my backyard Zen-like garden

My First MD Anderson Experience
jaw-dropping

And the Doctor said, "Very, very good results!"
33% reduction welcome

Back to Reality: 3C
Chemo Crushes Cancer

#8 Delayed
gastric issues rule

Back of Track #8
Chemo Crushes Cancer

#8 In progress Right Now!
grandkids rule

Mothers Will totally "Get It"
déjà vu of pregnancy days

A Glorious Day to Remember
11th grandchild arrives

Learning New Lessons Every Week!
my own fault

It's My Birthday!
69 and counting

T.G.I.F. – Another One
Colorado fires devastating

Back on Track with 3C Treatment
a gift that keeps on giving

My Really Good Week!
on our way to Camp Owen CO

Riding a Rocky Mountain High
keeping up with Steven and family

Bummer
luxuriating in our 'ether chairs'

The Blessings of Being in CO
*happiness is being with Jeff's family and
reconnecting with so many IBMers*

What a Beautiful Morning...
6 days without doctors

Last 3C day Before MD Anderson
summer CO days with Laney, Riley, and Ford

So Many Unexpected Issues
last time for freeze mode

It's a Great Day in Houston
looking to the future

The Skies Are Really Blue Again!
2-week vacation

Just Rockin' Along
and meeting with a medium

Back to Chemo Tomorrow...
and 2 weeks with Carson

Good News and a Little Bad News Today
Blake Owen Endowment
Dell Children's Medical Foundation
Attn: Susan Hewitt
4900 Mueller
Austin, TX 78723

Almost a Year
mental health and suicide prevention

Happy Anniversary to Us!
48 years of making history – what a story

Change of Plan
another Labor Day weekend

Moving Forward with Plan C
trying new chemo pills

Moving Past Mondays
a year like no other

Feeling Good and Going Back to Austin
doctors are my new family

And the Beat Goes On and On and On...
back to Arkansas from CO via Austin

Haven't Forgotten to Write
next stop: MD Anderson yet again

Great News!
Whoo Hoo! Glory to God!

Secret Revealed
cross my heart: dog-dewormer is a key part of my regimen

Preparing for a Joyous Christmas
Ho, Ho, Ho

Christmas Letter without Photos (sent previously)

2019

Couldn't Be More Grateful for Today's Great News!
bringing in the new year!

A Little Bump in the Road
no, no, no, bump, bump, bump

Keepin' On Bumpin' Along
a beautiful blue-sky day

A Tough One to Write
shaman diagnoses PTSD

A New Path Along the Journey
staying focused on my mental recovery

It's a Wonderful Life
stable sounds so good!

Things Not Going Too Well
infection not welcome

More Not so Good News
CEA and CA19-9 numbers rising dangerously!

Patience Is Not Always a Virtue
hear me roar

Anchored in Austin
cyber knife radiation delays trip to CO

Memorial Day – NOT
working with the interventional radiologist

Grit and Gratitude
rapid remodel of Owen lake cottage in Arkansas

Happy Independence Day 2019
fireworks and cyber knife radiation in Austin

Piece of Cake
painless, easy and uneventful treatment

Back to the Beginning
tumors growing again: NOT in the game plan

Just the Facts
back on the monster Fulfirinox

Gotta Do What I Gotta Do
I WILL WIN the Fulfirinox battle

One Week Down
double whammy takes its toll

More Than a Week's Reprieve
cyber knife machine takes a vacation

Back to Bald… and to Arkansas
2nd round of baldness

Some Labor Day Weekends Are Better Than Others
kids & grandkids make for a super holiday weekend

@#$%&*
bummer

The Good, the Bad, and the Hopeful
back to MD Anderson

Bump, Bump, Bump on This Winding Road
Mondays becoming Hump Days

Some Weeks Seem to Last Forever
laying of the hands miraculous

Doing the Happy Dance...sans Medical Boot!
Dr. Beck (Highlands Oncology Group) works a deal with Genentech

Godwinks in Abundance!
read Godwinks Stories

Loving the Fall Temps of AR
feautiful fall AR foliage, not so pretty pancreatic tumor

Double Whammy Takes Its Toll
hard work and determination to survive dual treatments

My Best Christmas Present
shrinking tumors for Christmas

Christmas Letter attached
The Owen family

2020

Ho Ho Ho Seems So Long Ago
a new year, a new decade

January 22, 2020: A Great Day
5-star rating

Celebrate! Celebrate! Dance to the Music!
potassium is important

More Tests of Faith
Lauren's 2nd big unexpected loss

My Membership to the Ultimate Spa
an unusual euphemism

Happy Valentine's Day
"The Oak Tree": a message of encouragement

4 Great Days and Counting
da, da, da, da, da, da, da, da = me singing

COVID-19 aka Coronavirus
the pandemic of our lifetime

Isolated in the Hospital – Surgery All Alone
scared and stressed

IF interested: All About Tomorrow's Surgery
medical lesson #?

Ever Slept Through the Nite in a Hospital?
freezing out a fever, stenting a clogged bile duct

Trial Failed
home in my big jacuzzi tub full of bubbles

Happy Monday Morning
What do you know about Bilirubin?

I Choose the JOY OF LIVING
life in the time of COVID-19

VHS - I Am Vital, Healty, Strong
my affirmations

Bald For the 3rd Time
glad to have Gary's laser machine back

Reprise: There's NO Place Like Home!
after 4.5 months in AR quarantine

June 11 – An Absolutely Fabulous 71st Birthday!
Steven & Shannon throw a drive birthday party

Shrinking, Shrinking, Shrunk! And the Winner is: K Sparky Strong
closing the 1st phase of my Bumpy Cancer Journey!

Can't Help Myself!
great drive-by celebration birthday video

FOREWORD

Have you ever been run over by the proverbial freight train? Karen and I were stopped cold in our tracks, reeling from the doctor's news.

"You have stage 4 pancreatic cancer that has metastasized in your liver. You may have as little as 3 weeks to live."

At a time when we needed to reduce the level of uncertainty, we were overwhelmed with medical jargon, unsure how to chose the best treatment options.

What would you do?

If you are Karen Owen, you write a book for the purpose of helping early-stage cancer patients remove the ambiguity she faced, so you, too, can live 3 quality years vs. 3 weeks. Because Karen loved life, she defied the doctor's original prediction and enjoyed the births of 2 more grandchildren and 60 family birthdays.

You also can achieve what Karen did... we hope with less stress and anxiety after reading this book.

Karen was by no means ordinary. She was 7th in her Chicago-area high school, magna cum laude, and the first one on either side of her family to graduate from college. After starting two businesses with me, she went back, at age 45, to school to get a OPM (Owner President Manager) degree from Harvard Business School, leaving me at home with five teenagers. Afterwards, she began a rewarding career at IBM, eventually rising to the role of Director of Education Worldwide Software.

Together we lived a no-limits life, facing challenges and making the most of our opportunities. And when family tragedies knocked her down, without fail, she got back up.

Karen hoped telling her story would help those who have been blindsided by a formidable foe, just as she was. She hoped her experience will remove much of the ambiguity of the enormous task ahead. She wanted you to know that cancer was not an immediate or inevitable death sentence and that you, too, can live to enjoy many more birthdays and anniversaries.

To my positive and loving soulmate for fifty-three years.

ILYF

Howard

STEP BY STEP
DAY BY DAY
one day at a time

My journey continues. The last three years have been life changing, and my spiritual journey has been challenging, touching, yet emotionally charged and so overwhelming. I cannot even fathom the number of prayer warriors who have prayed for me for three years now.

How can that be?

So this book is for you, and I hope you will gain an understanding of the concept of taking it one day at a time, trusting in the Lord, and knowing that Jesus Christ has a purpose for me – and for you.

The challenge is, I'd like to know what that purpose is. After 71 years of trying, it's hard to change that control, which has been to steer the Owen ship in the choppy waves.

I will continue to respond to the name my late friend Judy gave me: *K Sparky Strong*. I've earned the name. As I keep working to support others, I'll share some of the hard-learned lessons that I have uncovered over the last three years.

Judy, I will continue to make you proud.

I hope this book speaks for itself and that you, too, will benefit from all the lessons I have worked so hard to incorporate in my life. This is my gift to you.

My Story

I am a walking miracle. I view my life as before and after January 27, 2018. It was on that life-altering date that I was diagnosed with Stage 4 Pancreatic cancer that had already metastasized to my liver.

When I saw my first oncologist a few days later, he stated that I could have as little as three weeks to live. WOW! Talk about shock and awe...

But here I am, almost three years later, living a more constrained but full life within the context of my new 'normal'. In fact, the plan was for this journal to be published in celebration of Howard's and my 50th wedding anniversary (August 29, 1970), and I can share that I never expected to be able to wear the beautiful dress I recently purchased for the upcoming, intimate vow-renewal ceremony in front of our cherished family and closest friends.

But it is still a mystery to me how I got this awful, incurable disease. And how have I endured for the past 2+ years?

But let's back up for a minute...

I have had a super-busy, over-the-top life with my entrepreneurial, work-aholic husband Howard and our five now-adult children: Jeffrey, Steven,

Scott, Tiffany, and Blake. Friends and family alike would roll their eyes and shake their heads at Howard's antics and adventures with the kids. Howard oversaw FUN, which included skiing, ice skating, ATVs, boats, bikes hiking, fishing, turtle hunting, +++.

Though Austin is our home, Howard had bigger dreams, so we bought our Camp Owen Colorado home and drove up there (19 hours) three times each year from 1982 until recently. We wanted to ensure the kids grew up with every experience we could provide. To this day, they've spent only one Christmas without snow.

At the same time, Howard devoted himself to building our ever-dynamic businesses 'with no limits.' I like to say I became the Matriarch focusing on the kids. On Saturdays, we had to create flow chart carpools to all five kids' sporting events, activities, and birthday parties.

At the same time, I was side by side with Howard building our businesses, taking leadership roles in the non-profit community, and even went back to Harvard Graduate Business School when I was 45 (and left the kids with Howard). In 2018 I finished a rewarding career at IBM (Howard and I traveled the world as my global responsibilities took me to more than 50 countries.)

Time passed quickly, and our kids chose amazing spouses who in turn bestowed upon us the joys of grandchildren. We rumbled along with the ups and downs and challenges that every family navigates while I subconsciously buried continued stress and psychological exhaustion.

Kalen, Tiffany, Ethan, Kyle, Liam, Steven, Brazos, Shannon, Westyn, Carson, Riley,
Howard, Karen, Laney, Lisa, Ford, Jeff, Amelia, Scott, Liz
(not pictured Blake, Averie, and Aspen)

Then, on October 5, 2013, we experienced the first of four catastrophic events...

Howard and I had just flown back to Austin from our beloved Camp Owen Colorado (in Ridgway, CO) where we had made 15 years of memories with our own grown children and delightful grandchildren. Our son Scott and daughter-in-law Liz were at our Austin home preparing a from-scratch dinner for us to enjoy with their only child, our beautiful 16-month old granddaughter Averie.

Howard came home from the store and asked all three of us where Averie was, and the next thing I remember is Scott shouting Averie's name and

jumping into the swimming pool to grab her. I'll never be able to erase the visual of her little brown leather shoes on top of the water...

Despite heroic efforts by EMS, our ANGEL Averie joined our Heavenly Father that day. Howard and I soon sold the family home because I just couldn't live with the grief and nightmares. Scott and Liz barely functioned for the next year or two as we all tried to put our lives back together.

Life marches on, even when I wish it wouldn't, and I begged to escape the pain and grief for just a few minutes. After years of prayer, meditation, and therapy to recover from the horror of witnessing Averie's death and holding her cold little body in my arms almost seven years ago, I sensed we began to heal, though our hearts will never stop hurting and her absence in our lives will always elicit the physical pain of her loss.

I still talk to her and include her in all our family events. I will always feel the anguish of guilt, regret, what-ifs, and a mother's pain of watching her son and daughter-in-law try to move forward.

Yet Glory to God: He has blessed Scott and Liz with two beautiful, active children, Carson and Amelia.

Life changing event #2...

In 2000, Howard purchased a small, local manufacturing business, building salon furniture and all things needed in beauty salons and spas. He and our eldest son Jeff have built it into the largest beauty industry manufacturer in the U.S.

Then in 2016, a disgruntled ex-employee set our manufacturing plant on fire. While this incident is certainly minimal to the agony of Averie's passing, it took our son Jeffrey and Howard almost 2½ years to work with the insurance companies, engineers, subs, and vendors to rebuild our facilities while keeping Kaemark afloat.

When we held the reopening in spring of 2018, Howard and I were both physically and mentally exhausted. To say a family business consumes you is an understatement.

And again, I bore a really heavy load of stress and worry that continued to fill my life-capacity "bucket' for stress and grief.

With God's grace, we prevailed and thought the worst was behind us. And then the absolute worst hit us...

In 2017, we realized our youngest son Blake was suffering with mental illness that we later discovered was the result of the destruction of the synapses in his brain due to a prescription drug. That drug, SUBOXONE, had been touted as a miracle drug upon its release, but has now been identified as a killer drug that is more addictive than heroin.

On September 11, 2018, Lauren (Blake's wife) called me in CO and told me that Blake really needed me to fly back to Austin to help him get through the week of therapy, doctors' appointments, and the debilitating effects of the Suboxone. (Indivior, the manufacturer of Suboxone, has since pleaded guilty to a felony charge and agreed to pay $600 million to resolve criminal and civil liability. Its former CEO was sentenced to 6 months in prison and fined $600,000. This outcome is the largest of DOJ's opioid resolutions.)

That was a devastating and emotional week

as I watched my beautiful, successful youngest son descend into paranoia, depression, and a severe hopelessness that he would ever be himself again (which turned out to be medically correct). I witnessed his descent into hell right before my eyes.

It was obvious we needed to check Blake immediately into an institution where he could get relief and support. But it wasn't to be and on September 17, 2018, Blake took his own life.

Just when our family seemed to recover from Averie's drowning, we now had to contend with the horror of losing Blake, my youngest, the glue of our family, my soulmate, the newlywed. Words cannot describe the pain, anguish, loss, despair, guilt, as well as my body and mind's inability to 'deal' with yet another tragedy. Losing Blake exceeded my capacity.

A parent should not outlive her child; nor should any grandmother outlive her granddaughter. And having been present at both scarring events created a debilitating and complex grief that has often left me despondent (with PTSD) and dysfunctional.

And then disastrous event #4: my cancer diagnosis.

I had the greatest job at IBM. In January 2018, my team and I were delivering a sales training workshop when I started having sharp pain and difficulty breathing. I had previously experienced this and was told to go to physical therapy where their mantra was "No pain, no gain" – which was killing me.

By the next morning, I was back in Austin having tests. I'll never forget, at 4:00 PM Thursday, my doctor called and delivered the shocking news: "Stage 4 Pancreatic cancer. Get your affairs in order."

Talk about shock and awe, and fear, and panic, and… and… and…

Monday morning, I had my first appointment with Dr. Shimkus at Austin Cancer Center. Howard, Jeffrey, and Steven went with me. I vaguely recall Dr. S as very professional and direct. When Steven suggested we might wait to think about treatments options, Dr. S's message to Steven was, "Your mother may have as little as three weeks to live, but with immediate treatment, we may keep her alive up to eleven months." We were all speechless.

On February 18, I started my first series of the monster chemo drug Fulfirinox. After 6 months, my tumors had shrunk an average of 40%, but the cumulative side effects were literally killing me.

After Saluda didn't work for me (bad, bad side effects), I was identified as having a gene mutation that was causing my tumors to grow. Message to self: do more research on potential treatments and get out of 'the box' with both traditional and non-traditional treatments.

The following email to a fellow cancer patient illustrates all the different treatments I discovered and added to my out-of-the-box arsenal of potential treatments.

Hi Mike,

Sorry this has taken so long to send to you. We've had guests all week and I had chemo yesterday. I have thought of you often in the past few days and saw your comments on Caring Bridge. First, please give your mother a big hug for me. She has already lost a son, as I have, which gives us a special bond that only a mother in grief can understand.

I have Stage 4 pancreatic cancer that had metastasized to my liver even before I was diagnosed.

As I've chronicled in Caring Bridge, I engaged in the traditional treatments plus so much more. I will try to list them here so you and I can further explore what you are interested in.

- Chemo
- Fulfirinox – monster of all chemos with horrendous side effects. I've had 2 full rounds of this. #1 Feb.-Oct. 2018. I was off everything until my tumors grew back and had to go back on Fulfirinox from June-Dec. 2019.
- Herceptin/Perjeta- The Drs. did my gene study – I have a gene mutation and I'm HER2 Positive which is the reason my tumors keep growing back. This treatment of Herceptin/Perjeta that I started in Dec. 2019 was supposed to stop tumor regrowth. It has been FDA approved for breast, colon and types of digestive cancers, so I am actually in a trial to see if it can work for pancreatic cancer. Have you heard of Herceptin? If you are experiencing tumor regrowth, you might ask your Dr about Herceptin if you haven't discussed it already. Also, watch the movie "Living Proof" (2009) with Robert Downey, Jr. It is the story of the development and approval of Herceptin – and how many lives it has saved. It was originally only for breast cancer, but they are testing for broader effectiveness. Unfortunately, it did NOT work for me. So onward...
- Watch the movie *HEAL*
- Nutrition – I have started working with Jim Judd who owns Nutritional Profiles out of Dallas. I do all my comms with him by phone and email. He specializes in supplements for oncology patients based on your specific blood test results. I suggest going to his website: Nutritionalprofiles.com. He has a huge group of cancer patients for whom traditional treatments have failed.
- Exercise – I don't do as much as I should, but I know it is important.
- Prayer – and for me, redefinition of my beliefs and relationship with God. And so much prayer – yours and your support groups.
- Meditation – I'm not too good at this, but I think Meditation is essential. Order and listen to the CD "A Meditation to Help You Fight Cancer" from healthjourneys.com (800-800-8661) This has been very helpful to me.

- Music Therapy – Pound out dissonant chords on the piano about 15 minutes per day. The theory is tumors will start to shrink in response to the non-melodic sounds. Also, listen to Gregorian Chant.
- Panacur C (dog dewormer) – I've been doing this for 2 years. Go to the website "Mycancerstory.rocks"
- Shaman – I go to a shaman and have my Shakras cleansed and realigned.
- Therapy – My therapist and Bible Study group both share so many books about God, cancer, etc.
- I have a whole new view to self-forgiveness, trying not to live in the guilt and grief of the past, not try to control the future, but to trust in God's plan and life each day to its max.
- Alkaline chemistry – I try to minimize acidic foods, etc. I also drink Alkaline water to move my Ph to the alkaline side.

I'll try to remember what else I've done before we talk, but I am also interested in all you've done... Let me know when you can talk.

> With love,
> Karen

After eight months being OFF treatment, by May 2019, my tumors were growing back, and I went for my 2nd round of Fulfirinox and Cyber Knife Radiation. Success again, but horrible side effects.

By Christmas, I was finishing my cycle of Fulfirinox, and started a trial of Herceptin/Perjeta to ascertain if this treatment could eradicate my HER2 Positive gene mutation and therefore stop the recurring tumor growth. In late March 2020, my cancer had spread to my lymph nodes and lungs, so no more Herceptin trial. Next up, a Phase 2 Pancreatic Trial focused on tumor reduction; this trial was not successful, so was not an option for me.

In May 2020, I started an alternative chemo treatment: Gemzar/Abraxane. Next CT scan to determine efficacy of this chemo cocktail was June 24, 2020 - ... and I am now in a very unusual state of "remission" that is very rare for stage 4 pancreatic cancer patients.

Fighting cancer is a full-time and exhausting job. Early on, I was so grateful and humbled by the hundreds of prayer warriors who supported and continue to support me. They have been a big part of my focus on my relationship with God, and the faith, hope, and love I have experienced and hope to pass on.

My growing and evolving relationship with God continues to be central to my ongoing journey, as reflected in my Caring Bridge journals sharing my

2½-year cancer challenge. I've often been told my journals have been inspirational and have changed many peoples' lives.

I am not the same Karen I was six, four, or two years ago. I am better. This change has allowed me to continue to research, try non-traditional treatments, counsel other cancer patients, and share my story. Through my words and actions, I am dedicated to inspiring and helping others (both sick and well) in praise of God and His gift of extending my life.

I know absolutely, positively that I am NOT in CONTROL – and that's a difficult concept to ingest and live.

My life has been so influenced by the love, support, prayer, cards, gifts and encouragement that so many have bestowed on me. I had NO IDEA. And now I want to share with you. I've been given as much as I have given and will continue to give.

I hope and pray that my Journal is my legacy to you. As Thomas Kincaid said, "Our most important legacy will be the contributions we make to the lives of other human beings."

My writing is raw and honest, and mirrors each step of my journey. I'm always willing and ready to bring solace and counsel to help others with all I have to give: "There but for the grace of God go I."

> With love and gratitude,
> Karen Sparky Strong
> (You'll have to read ahead to discover how I earned this name!)

Note: As you read my story, wonderful family and friend supporters have sent thoughtful comments in response to each journal. Rather than publish all the many loving but repetitive comments, I have selected a few unique and special comments to publish with each Journal entry.

At each Journal entry, I have also called out the main message of that entry so you can focus on what is of most interest to you each day. Your greatest gift to me would be to make my legacy come to life through YOU.

2018

THE BEGINNING OF
MY UNEXPECTED JOURNEY
where to begin

"NEVER, EVER FORGET that you are an amazing, strong, brave, loving, intelligent, committed, talented, adventurous, fun-loving, one-of-a-kind woman..."
Marlene

February 6, 2018

Dearest family and friends,

I wish you weren't receiving this, but... As you know, the last 4½ months since we lost Blake have been the most painful, grief-filled days of our lives. Blake's death was the third tragedy of our four-year journey of grief, loss and stress.

Our beautiful 16-month-old granddaughter, Averie, drowned in our swimming pool four years ago. Then three years ago, an arsonist burned down our manufacturing plant - and Howard and son Jeff spent 2½ years rebuilding and keeping us afloat (the reopening was May 2017). Then the worst of all, we lost our Blake to suicide last September.

The grief, loss, and stress have taken their toll, and I've just been diagnosed with stage 4 pancreatic and liver cancer. If I do chemo (which I will), the doctor is giving me 12-18 months. If not, 2-3 months. But you all know I'm a fighter, so...

Please keep me and my family in your positive thoughts and prayers. Also, I can't do this alone - please stay in touch and help fill my days with humor. I need to laugh and smile. I hardly remember what that is.

Either I or my kids will be adding updates to this site. I've decided this is the only way I'll be able to keep up. We are currently so overwhelmed with everything.

With love - and great fear,
Karen

"My heart aches for you and your family.
Everyone is different and responds differently to treatment
You may be the patient they talk about 10 years from now and
how you beat the odds. Everyone loves you, Karen,
and if the number of prayers for you makes a
difference, then you're the winner. Love to you."
Jo Lynne

PROGRESS
just getting started

"You inspire me everyday. Love you, Mom!"
- Liz O

February 11, 2018

The last few weeks since we received my shocking diagnosis have been fast and furious. The imminent result is that I am starting chemo tomorrow morning.

Really can't write more than that at the moment. Too scared - but I'll let you know how things are going.

love, K

"You looked so beautiful in your red outfit surrounded by
all of your grandkids. Praying for your peace and strength,
and for wisdom and compassion for your medical team
as you start treatment today. Love you."
Lisa

FIRST CHEMO
first lesson of cancer

"We're all with you every step of the way,
any time of night or day.
Head up and march on, my friend.
We've got your back! xoxo"
Pam

February 13, 2018

It is now midnight, so I'll give you a quick update and write more tomorrow. A pretty good first chemo day. Some little, fixable glitches, but overall good. I was disappointed to learn that my liver enzymes are so high, they had to reduce the potency of my chemo cocktail by 25%. Also, my bio-marker excluded me from getting a breakthrough drug (only 12% are compatible). Onward with existing course.

Sleep well, K

"Did you name your port?
Look at it as your best friend that will
kill/control that DAMN cancer!
Give it a hopeful or a badass name."
Deb

HAPPY WEEKEND!
balancing a gyroscope

"Love this attitude and sense of fight in you!
You have always been my hero
and the sister I lacked.
Crappy cancer has never tangled with Karen Owen,
and my money is wagered on you!
You will kick cancer's ass to the curb!"
Fran

February 17, 2018

I have great intentions to write every day, but alas, we have been sooo busy and by 7 PM each night, I'm pretty fatigued. I have been very lucky in that I haven't had any side effects from Monday's chemo until tonight. Hopefully, it won't get much worse because I'm still feeling pretty good. Big blessings.

So much has happened. The noted Dr. Milind Javle of MD Anderson in Houston has accepted me as a patient. (Thank you. brother Gary!) We'll find out this week how soon he'll see me, but from what I understand, he wants to wait until I finish my first three months of chemo; then I'll go to Houston for the next CT and other tests.

Additionally, I have spent several hours with IBM Watson oncology. They will feed my data into Watson Monday/Tuesday and then discuss my best treatments based on thousands of others like me.

Next, they will also recommend the best clinical trials within 250 miles of Austin that would match my criteria. Then I hope to participate in Watson genomics to identify my genetic markers to analyze my tumors. That could lead to a plethora of new options - immunotherapy, +++. Please pray for positive results...

I guess this journey will be like trying to balance a gyroscope. This week I've developed anemia, so back to get an infusion of iron Monday. I don't know what I'd do without my amazing kids, my daughters-in-law, and all my wonderful supportive friends.

I honestly believe your loving, ongoing outreach and prayers will sustain me.

xo, K

(l-r) Kathy G, Cindy B, Sydney J,
Sandy P, Mary Gay G, Karen O

"Nothing you do EVER surprises me!
You have the most indomitable spirit I have ever known
(other than my mom). If attitude and determination,
plus prayers and family/friends count,
you are unbeatable. Love you…"
Jeani

AND ONE MORE DIET TIP
broccolini, bok choy in my backyard

"Ohhhhhh good!!!
Your diet sounds much like mine,
which started last May and saved my life.
Not an ounce of exaggeration here.
When I see my nutritionist, I want to genuflect!!"
Alegria

February 18, 2018

Thank you to Shannon's brother, Kelly Logue, and to Amy, who brought me a whole tray of their broccolini, which is supposed to be super-charged to fight pancreatic cancer. They also brought me their nutritious home-grown organic lettuces and bok choy.

Karen Owen going out on to her patio and cutting the broccolini right off the roots? Who woulda thunk? Wonders never cease!

Thanks and love to all, K

"Your posts inspire me to improve my diet,
and my attitude in general.
I have so much to learn from you!"
Gail

IT'S HARD WORK
this is harder than my full-time job at IBM

"Side effects are good! That means it's working!"
Kathy

February 20, 2018

I can't believe how slow but how fast the days are passing - sounds like a contradiction, but that's how it seems. We have so much information and so many requirements for each contact, it is a full-time job to keep up with everything. I'm not complaining, since so many people have reached out with the best contacts in the country - both traditional treatments and 'alternatives' - but still overwhelming.

Before we start taking advantage of MD Anderson, Ohio State, Baylor Med, etc., I have to complete four rounds of chemo - which means patience (one of my shortcomings). We've also considered so many 'alternative' treatments, but I think we'll wait until I get to MD Anderson and see how I'm doing before we try other options.

I've had a few mild side effects over the last few days, but it reminds me of all those days of pregnancy - and God knows, I had "a few" of those! The joyous results of those pregnancies are my wonderful children! I have faith the challenges of chemo will result in my longer, healthy life!

I've also started meditating - another whole new learning experience for me. But very importantly, part of that visualization includes all of you in your support of me. So selfishly, please keep me in your thoughts and prayers.

One unavoidable side effect is fatigue, and I have it in spades. Hope it doesn't last - really cramping my style!

Love to all, K

"I know Blake is cheering you on from above.
By the way, it is time Howard learned some household chores.
He has had it way too easy.
I hope sunshine greets you in the morning. Love ya!"
Fran

Guess I'm a 2nd Weeker...
and full-time member of "cancer club"

"We will get sunshine again... it is Texas...
and in the meantime, consider all the love and prayers
coming your way as your Vitamin D. xoxo"
Kim H

February 21, 2018

As you know, I sailed through the first week after my first chemo and thought, "Hey, this isn't so bad."

Alas, the chemo goblin got me. Pretty rough night last night, and then I've been so lightheaded, I fainted this morning. Fainting is a new experience for me and I'd rather not do it again...

Bless Howard: he is getting a full indoctrination. He has learned to load and turn on the dishwasher (and does dishes daily), he now knows how to use the washer and dryer, and he has become very familiar with Whole Foods.

He is the consummate chauffeur, caregiver, and soulmate. We are running around the city almost daily for tests, doctor appointments, meds. And that's how he is spending his first month of retirement. Not quite what we had in mind for our golden years, but we're looking forward to days beyond chemo and all that entails.

I was coming to the Infusion lab (where they do all IV stuff) for IV iron today, but as soon as I got here, they ran labs and decided to give me IV fluids. Now we're waiting to see what else they want to push in my IV.

So another day in these big leather chairs, looking at the rainy, cloudy weather outside. I sure am ready for some sunshine - need my dose of natural vitamin D.

I sit here and wonder about the stories of all those around me. There are six of us in here this afternoon (the mornings are usually busier). Three appear older, two look to be my age, and one is younger. I've become a member of too many undesirable 'clubs' in the last 4 years... and now I find myself in yet another one. I'm paying my dues for long-term membership!

A day doesn't go by that we don't love and miss our Blaker. We've survived so many 'firsts' in our grief journey over the five months since that horrible day, September 17. I'm working very hard to shift my thinking, grieving, and go-forward relationship with Blake.

I know that he is with me - and I believe he is holding my hand throughout my chemo treatments. I feel so close to him, knowing he is always in my heart. It is still so hard, but I know he will be with me through this entire journey - and we're only at the starting line!

> More to come...
> Love, K

"Love you, friend!! Starting line is correct,
all of us wishing you an Olympic run!!"
Mary Gay

GRATEFUL FOR BETTER DAYS
still in research mode

"So good to see you have Avenging Angels,
otherwise known as daughters-in-law...
Feed those healthy cells.
Have a glass of red wine,
and use the good crystal."
Mary C

February 23, 2018

I had a great day yesterday - and feel good again today (Friday). I walked three-quarters of a mile, and Howard and I are off to do it again this morning. And I know this is the power of YOU! - so keep it up because I'm seeing results.

Have a great weekend. I'll be having chemo Monday, courage needed! I'll let you know how it goes. My doctor is quite a well-known pancreatic oncologist, so fingers crossed he has some positive things to convey. Hopeful.

xo, K

"Awesome !!!
Walking is awesome...
so is your positive attitude.
You are an inspiration !!!"
Janie C

THE MOST MEMORABLE AFTERNOON
"Damn Joy" party

"I was so sad to miss! But what kind of friend would I be if I gave you a cold??? :-(
Your great friends are just paying back all the love
and friendship you have extended over the years."
Kathy

February 24, 2018

What a fabulous, memorable, once-in a lifetime "Damn Joy" party yesterday afternoon. Two of my best friends, Sandy P and Deb G, decided to throw an intimate celebration for my best 'through thick and thin' friends.

Wow! What a unique, life experience that I will cherish forever. I had no idea how much love, support, and respect these incredible women could bestow on me. If I weren't gung-ho before, I sure came away with a can-do, go-forward attitude.

From Sandy's food and delectable desserts (especially her incomparable chocolate cake), to colorful feather boas, decorated surgical masks, funny animals, flowers - and most importantly, a letter/note/story/ poem that each friend wrote personally to me to add to my notebook.

Oh, the messages - wow! Dearest girlfriends and daughter/in-laws - I LOVE YOU - thank you all for such an honor! Deb and Sandy - you outdid yourselves.

To top it off, Karen C. had all my international travel journals that I wrote to family and friends from 2008-2016 printed and assembled in a binder. Much to my surprise, I wrote a book! The binder is 2" thick of 8.5x11" paper - unedited. So I may actually need to edit these musings into a logical book.

I want to thank all of you for your texts, cards, emails, phone messages. I do believe your ongoing support will help see me through.

xo, K

"It is no surprise to me how much you are loved! Sending big hugs your way."
Barbara N

ANOTHER MONDAY BUMP
IN THE ROAD
followed by a wig shop visit, not a bar?

"Turbans can be stylish, and they don't itch!!
You are beautiful with or without hair!!"
Alegria

February 26, 2018

Friday was a glorious day. Then Saturday I found out my neighbor, who also has pancreatic cancer, discovered his cancer has spread into his lymph nodes. Sunday my hair started falling out.

This morning, Liz, my dear daughter-in-law, went with me to chemo, and when we got there, my doctor said my blood cell count is so low that we couldn't do chemo. So they're treating me with all kinds of things every day this week. Hopeful we'll be back on track next Monday.

After the morning at the doctor's office, Liz and I ventured out to the wig shop. What a hoot.

"Cannot wait to see what you pick.
I am going for a red head."
Penny P

GOOD NEWS ABOUT KAREN!
+60 lbs. ago with my own hair

"OMG - Did Howard cut her hair? I love the new look!"
Fran

February 28, 2018

"Love the new 'do'!!"
Anna S

STARVING
now I'm a TX criminal, too

"CBD oil is effective in many ways...
If it eliminates or alleviates pain or anxiety for you
during this, you have all of my blessings. xoxo"
Kim H

March 4, 2018

Gearing up for chemo tomorrow, and I have to fast for 24 hours before chemo, so I'm listening to my stomach growl at me. But that's okay, my digestive system is glad to have a break from doing its thing, and I'm enjoying the relief from the pain. I just had a four-day vacation from doctors, and it was so nice. Thursday and Friday are the first two weekdays since my diagnosis with no appointments. I feel like I'm on vacation.

We continue to research and uncover new medical trials. And I'm sticking to my meditation and restrictive diet. (As challenging as this diet is, my fear of introducing the 'old' food back into my diet is frightening.) So onward...

I'm also going to be taking CBD Oil with THC. Have any of you heard of this or tried it?

At the moment, I am soooo sleepy, I'm falling asleep sitting up. So more later.

Have fun watching the Academy Awards tonight!

It Must Be Monday
from short to gone

"Come on, Sunshine!!!! Can't help but believe God has a reason for the chemo delays!!!... I welcome the abundance of wholeness and healing!! Thank you, God!"
Alegria

March 5, 2018

Back at the Infusion lab. And guess what? I have a different issue that will require some additional scans today, so they are scheduling those scans asap - which means no chemo again today. If they get good scan results back late today, we'll try to do chemo tomorrow... Very frustrating - remember, we had to cancel chemo last week, too.

At the same time, my cute little short haircut is not so cute any more. My beautiful head of hair has deserted me. So I'm going to try to get my head shaved today after my scans.

While this is one of the least of my current challenges, it's an emotional situation. Another reality check. I must admit, my mood is reflecting the dreary weather outside.

It was a very long awake night (though I did get 3-4 hours sleep), and in the dark of night, it is so difficult to control your thoughts and emotions. Bless Howard for being up with me when missing Blake is so debilitating for both of us. We have to believe he is better now, but he did leave such a void. I truly believe he is helping me now and will be walking next to me on this bumpy journey.

I'll let you know how things shape up later - and if I'll be able to go back to chemo tomorrow. Fingers crossed.

xo, K

"Must be positive thinking because the sun just came out!!! We are all supporting you with uplifting vibes. You have such courage."
Mary Gay

AND IT WAS THE LONGEST MONDAY
can't always count on your GPS

"A tough story, but it's like I'm hearing your voice,
beautifully written, clear and poetic!
Write more, love reading your words, your truth, your life."
Beatriz F

March 6, 2018

Sometimes I wonder at the relativity of time - some days are so fast and furious and some never end. That was my day yesterday. Once we discussed the significant digestive track pain I had been in over the weekend, no chemo and Plan B.

I was alone yesterday because Howard didn't feel well in the morning, and we decided he shouldn't be close to me, and certainly not in the infusion lab. So off I went at 7:15 AM for what I thought was going to be a normal chemo day.

Fast forward, it is now 11:00 AM and PA Rachel says, "You need to be at St. David's Surgical Hospital at noon for CT and x-ray.".

So off I go, knowing the GPS says it is only 15 minutes away from the Infusion Lab. Well, my new short do was no longer doing, so I decided to stop at my Wig Lady's shop and have her shave my head - OMG! The outcome was quite a shockeroo.

But okay, I bought a cute little Mao-type hat, covered my lily-white scalp skin, and off I went to St. David's in Round Rock. I'm quite adept at GPS, but 30 minutes later, both Waze and Google maps have dumped me in an open field looking at huge storage units.

I'm sweating now. I'm panicking because I can't miss my tests. I call the hospital and they put me through to the security guard, whose GPS does the same thing as mine. He scrambled to find a good old-fashioned map and became my live navigator to the hospital.

I finally arrived 40 minutes after my appointment time - and as I walked in, the receptionist, security guard, scrub nurse all say, "Yeah, that happens at least once a week." The physical address and mailing address don't match and although the address is Round Rock, it is really Austin. But, they were very kind, I got my tests and headed for home to wait for results.

At 4 PM, I got the call. I have diverticulitis (didn't know that) and one of the sacs are now abscessed. So PA Rachel instructs me to go directly to St. David's ER - she will have talked to the doctor in advance of my arrival, because we don't have any time to lose to get this infection under control.

Arrived at ER around 6 (lovely crossing Austin in rush hour). After much ado drawing blood, drawing more blood, and drawing more blood, and flooding my system with fluids to ward off sepsis, they decide they need a specialist to stick a needle into the abscessed sac and drain the infection over the next 4-5 days.

Alas, not to be. The abscess is wedged between my bladder and vagina, and the risk of getting to the abscess is too risky. So I'm at St. David's for the week (???), where they are flooding me with antibiotics to try to kill the abscess. We won't know if this will work for at least a few more days. Then another CT scan and ???

To sleep at night, they are giving me morphine - yikes. I just told the doctor I don't want to take morphine during the day, but she said it is very important NOT to be in pain so my body can fight the infection and not the pain. So we're going to try tramadol during the day. Hope it works.

Red alert - my blood pressure is spiking, so now they need to figure out what to do about that... the gyroscope is out of control.

Sorry if this is TMI but so many of you are asking for 'more meat' than what I've been writing. There, you've got it. Read at your own risk.

Dear friends/family, please up the prayers to get rid of this infection so I can get back to chemo and overcome the ugly cancer demon.

Still hard to believe this journey started on February 9... we will reach 1 month this Friday.

Love and appreciate you, K

"Well, that was a Monday to beat all Mondays!!!
Congratulations on making it through!! So many bumps in the road...
You are in good hands. I hope your Tuesday is better."
Kathy

Hump Day Update
remember those college days?

"Gahhh, long day! I had no idea.
Now I know why I was thinking about you all day.
Love the updates. Not TMI! We want it all!
Thanks, Mom. Love you!"
Jenny B Q

March 7, 2018

So you ask - Hump Day? Don't you remember Wednesday nights in college? Wednesday was always celebration night that you had made it

half way through the week. I do remember lots of fun Wednesday nights with a slow gin fizz and dancing the night away... with Howard, of course.

But this hump day is so much different. The last thing the surgeon said to me yesterday was, "Let's delay the surgery to drain the abscess for 24 hours and see if the abscess will start draining itself".

And, lo and behold, the abscess was draining this morning and has continued all day. Thank the Lord for this gift.

Not out of the woods yet.

Had a fever last night and white blood cell count is 14K. They won't let me leave until white blood cell count is under 10K, no fever for 24 hours - AND continued improvement with IV meds and then with oral antibiotics. As of now, I'll be going home Saturday or Sunday with orders to finish a 14-day supply of meds. Then, hope we'll get back to the priority of chemo and chasing those cancer cells OUT and AWAY.

SO many dear friends visited me yesterday and today - and all I can say, is THANKS, GIRLFRIENDS, for spending time with me - and for the great goodies. You make all the difference to me, and Howard thanks you for relieving him; this hospital stuff all day is just not in his DNA.

Love, K

"Hump and dip, hump and dip, dip and hump…
a bit like a roller coaster!
Hard to maintain equilibrium.
But congratulations on figuring out
how to go with the flow!
Not that I am surprised."
Kathy

There's No Place Like Home
beautiful scarves will sustain

"On to Shanghai. Will find you a beautiful scarf-
what color would you like? …
Positive baby steps become positive bigger steps.
Stay strong and positive. Love you."
Susan W

March 9, 2018

The doctors dismissed me from the hospital yesterday afternoon. Glory be! I am so glad to be home. I'm now on a round of 11 more days of antibiotics - and then should be able to restart chemo around March 22.

Thank you to all who sent beautiful flowers, which made my room smell and look like spring in full bloom.

And to my dear friends who answered Sandy's call: Thank you for all the beautiful scarves - I will remember each of you when I wear them - from the 70s retro scarves to the latest from Chanel.

I love you all and the beautiful symbols of your love and concern for me. I appreciate the daily cards, books, prayers, emails - and those grocery runners, those who help keep me organized - and so much more.

As I meditate each morning, you are all in the group I see surrounding me and cheering me on. Your support and prayers are making all the difference.

I get down and wouldn't be able to get back up without you. So don't let up -

Love y'all, K

"So glad to hear you are home!
Make sure Howard caters to your every need!
It is about time the roles are reversed. Love ya!"
Fran B

A GREAT SATURDAY
afternoon on NIRVANA

"Sounds like you had a wonderful time on the lake!
So special to hear.
Good luck tomorrow, fingers crossed."
Barbara N

March 11, 2018

I feel so good since I came home. It was 88 degrees and sunny Saturday, so we spent the afternoon on NIRVANA - you ask, *what is Nirvana?*

It's our wonderful boat on Lake Travis. And the name is very important and was carefully chosen. We always have a great time and yesterday we had Jeff, Lisa, Laney and Riley with us. The girls even jumped in the water - bbrrrr - with Papa's bribe of money if they would stay in 20 seconds - AND they did it.

We went to our favorite restaurant on the lake called Rough Hollow and experienced the most beautiful sunset (Colorado quality). A great day all day long!

The week I was diagnosed (Feb. 9 - seems like years ago), Kirk Boothe, a great guy who was on my IBM team and often traveled with me during my international travel years, reached out to me since he had been diagnosed with stage 4 pancreatic cancer a month before me. We quickly resumed our relationship and compared notes every few days - the side effects of the chemo, etc., etc.

When I came home from the hospital Thursday, he had not emailed, so I sent him a note right away, only to have the email bounce back. Looked him up online, and discovered he had passed. I reached out to his son who responded right away.

I mention this because Kirk's quick demise had a very scary impact on me. I also want to pay tribute to a wonderful man who was so giving that he asked his son to reach out to me the day before he died. I am so sad for his family... and still have to process. I've added Kirk to my heavenly support group and know he will do everything in his power to encourage me.

"Rest in everlasting peace and happiness with the Lord, Alabama boy.
I will miss you!"

Correction from Friday: Karen C. and Deb G. were the initiators of the "Call for Scarves" Wow! These women are effective. Scarves galore at my fingertips to satisfy every whim!

Thank you all, dear friends. Not only am I grateful and touched, but Howard is amazed at my wonderful 'army' of love and support - not only for scarves, but for so much more.

I go for more blood work tomorrow. Keep fingers crossed for good numbers!

Love, K

"Your friend will be your heavenly angel
as you begin your journey."
Fran

GONNA BE AN INTENSE WEEK
Watson Oncology results

"My heart is cheering your heart on. May grace be your constant gift!"
Janie C

March 12, 2018

It's Monday again, and Mondays have started falling into the category of 'the most challenging day of the week.'

What's good? My blood work is good today, so we're starting chemo again tomorrow. Then Tuesday chemo, the external port until Thursday - and then a nupagen shot on Friday... that's the one to bring up my white blood cell count that made me so sick several weeks ago. This time I'm going to be better prepared in advance...

We're leaving for my brother Glen's daughter's wedding in Dallas Friday afternoon. I'm determined to feel good all weekend! We should arrive just in time for the rehearsal dinner! Can't wait.

So what's disappointing? We had our consultation to discuss the results of Watson Oncology this afternoon. Despite running my data through Watson data leveraging AI, my results came back that the Fulfirinox chemo that I'm on is what they recommend and basically there's nothing else they suggested. They didn't even think trials would help.

So I'm really bummed. All the hype about Watson, and no new recommendations or a pathway to new treatments. Ramp up the prayers that the Fulfirinox works on my tumors because the alternatives are limited. (We won't know until after my fourth infusion of Fulfirinox if it works for me - and I'm doing the second one tomorrow.)

Anyway, it is a beautiful day. After we went to the doctor this morning, we walked around Northside at the Domain and had lunch at Flower Child, a chic new healthy food restaurant. It was packed - healthy eating must be "in," and it was really good, too.

Aren't you loving being back on Daylight Savings Time? Enjoy!
Love, K

"Do well today.
I hate Mondays, too!"
Jenny B

"You go, girl! Keep kicking abscess ass and taking names!
Sending you love and hugs from Chi-town! xoxo"
Rachel K

"Continued prayers.
You're an inspiration and have many villages praying for you.
I hope to hug you this weekend. We love you!"
Kathleen B

A Wonderful Weekend at Lizzie's Fairy Tale Wedding
from a horse-drawn carriage arrival to a fireworks departure - and everything in between

"Sounds fabulous.
Enjoy the day, it is truly beautiful!"
Anna S

March 19, 2018

I had a really good week last week and enjoyed a fabulous time in Dallas at my niece Lizzie's wedding this past weekend. Oh what a wedding it was. Glen and Patty hosted the most beautiful, over-the-top, princess wedding imaginable.

Envision Lizzie and Glen's arrival in a horse-drawn carriage through fireworks at the end of the evening – and every dazzling detail in between: an event not to be forgotten. And we all had the most wonderful time! A complete memory-making weekend for all. I'm so happy I was able to make the trip.

Today, I went for my blood work check-up, and I'm back to the daily nupagen shots this week to build up my white blood cell count. But that's okay. I still feel good and the weather is gorgeous. Keeping fingers crossed that I don't have the bad side effects from the nupagen. So far, so good!

I'll let you know how things are progressing through the week - but as far as I'm concerned, no news is good news, so we're going to proceed with no new news!

Love, Karen

"I watch *The Voice* and Kelly Clarkson's voice and
outgoing personality remind me so much of you.
I pray for you every time she talks!
Hope all goes well on Monday!"
Amy

T.G.I.F.
no news is good news?

"Your positive outlook is an inspiration for all.
Do not give up.
Miracles are all around us!
I love you, my friend!"
Lynn N

March 23, 2018

Happy Friday! Have you missed me this week? Actually, no news is good news this week. I've made it through my week of nupagen shots and have felt good all week. In fact, I've felt good for 2 weeks now - and it has been great! Now I'm right on schedule for chemo Monday morning.

Here's hoping for another two weeks of getting treatment AND feeling good.

We've now scheduled our visit to MD Anderson on Thursday, April 19. We need to be there for three-four days, but during our time there, we will find out if my current chemo regimen is working or not.

Fingers crossed.

I so strongly believe all your prayers and positive thoughts have helped bring me to this beautiful, pain-free Friday, so please don't stop now. We have a long way to go, and I'm taking it one day at a time. Next hurdle: MD Anderson.

Have a great weekend,

Karen

"Great news! Have a relaxing weekend and
conquer Monday like a rock star!
Always in my prayers! Love you."
Fran

IT'S TRIPLE C DAY!
Triple c = chemo crushes cancer Day

"We hold you in prayer each day
(Shirley would be proud of her problem child)
and know the chemo will be very beneficial.
Have a restful night's sleep tonight
and be strong tomorrow."
Mark and Betsy

March 26, 2018

You may ask, "Karen, what in the world is TRIPLE C day?"

Well, I've coined a new expression: TRIPLE C days are my chemo infusion days, and I choose to call them Chemo Crushes Cancer days. Yes, I had a good TRIPLE C day today!

We started the day at 8:15 by drawing blood for my current counts. Then we met with my oncologist, who was very pleased that all my counts are 'in the boundaries,' a successful TRIPLE C day.

Now I'm home with my external pump that will continue to infuse more cancer attack drugs for another 2 days. BUT I feel good - da da dadadada (That's me singing again).

And what do you know? Since I'm feeling so good, Howard is feeling much better, too - and his knees are not even hurting any more. How's that for transference after being married 48 years...

As many of you know, March 17 was the six-month anniversary of Blake's death. On that day, we were in Dallas at my niece Lizzie's wedding. While we had a wonderful time sharing in her beautiful, joyful day, inside we struggled with missing our beloved Blake.

Since the 17th, it has been so hard to refocus on my positive outlook; I've gone back to focusing on one day at a time and trying to control my thoughts and emotions - so difficult with the continuing heart-shattering grief for Blake.

Yet every day, I receive beautiful gifts, cards notes, and Caring Bridge comments from so many of you. I CAN"T even begin to tell you how much this means to me. I truly believe your prayers are helping me to compart-mentalize my grief, and I appreciate all the positive love and support coming from so many directions.

In fact, in my meditations, I envision all of you surrounding me as I work hard to leverage my body's healing power to rid it of cancer cells. That can only happen with God's help - and I know he is hearing all your prayers. I am also truly feeling your support.

Love, Karen

"I can hear you singing from here.
So glad for the good test results and
your dedication to positive thoughts, even in your grief.
Hang in there,
and continued prayers heading your way!"
Sharon

"Triple C attacking - STRONG. Karen, STRONG - not surprised.
My prayers call your name every day."
Judy W

Judy W & Karen

A New Normal
positive attitude and prayer

"You have such a beautiful energy in your words.
Keep up the fight,
you are stronger than you think!"
Beatriz F

March 29, 2018

This week has been pretty emotional. Howard and I went to put fresh flowers on Averie's and Blake's graves last Saturday, and my positive attitude and hard work over the last seven weeks dissipated under the resurgent grief and loss of my cherished son and my beautiful granddaughter.

At the same time, I'm just beginning to realize that this cancer will be the focus of my life for the duration. I'm at the doctor's office almost every day, and each time I go, they end up giving me a new IV bag of something my body is lacking (potassium this week) - what a gyroscope.

The good thing is that my doctor and his team are monitoring my blood work at least three times each week. I am confident they are on top of things. Maybe I'll get a job in that office because I'm there so much. (-:

We've had to push my MD Anderson appointment back to end of May because of my interrupted chemo schedule. But that's okay. I'm sort of getting into the routine and trying to focus on one day at a time. I'm determined to get my mojo back because I truly believe a positive attitude and prayer have already made a difference. I guess I have to embrace my new normal - whatever that may be.

It is a beautiful, warm sunny day. We just came back from Grandparents' Day with Laney and Riley and are heading out to the lake for the afternoon. *That* will help me regain my equilibrium and positive attitude, if anything can.

Have a blessed and wonderful Easter weekend. Eat some chocolate eggs for me!

xo, K

"Enjoy the lake on this beautiful day!
The sunshine always lifts my spirits.
Every thing is growing, turning green,
and renewing to greet the Spring.
Blessings."
Anna S

"You are an inspiration. Your incredibly strong spirit,
positive attitude, strong sense of faith mixed in
with good dose of stubbornness combined with
the love of your family and friends is a formidable mixture
to you get thru each day as you are dealing with the "new normal".
Happy Easter to you and yours!"
Lynn T

Riley, Ford, and Laney

So Grateful for Beautiful Weather
Happy Easter

"Drinking in the wildflowers
and all this lovely sunshine should be lifting!!!
R & R with nature is a winning combination!!
Perfect way to spend Easter."
Mary Gay

April 2, 2018

What a wonderful Easter weekend - four days of glorious weather, family, fun - and feeling good! I guess all good things must end because today was a typical Monday for me. Had to go in to the doctor first thing this morning for blood work; lo and behold, my white cell count is at the bottom of the barrel again and my platelets seemed to have abandoned me, too.

So nupagen shots every day this week again to help me tolerate the chemo next Monday. The biggest issue is that the shots propelling my body to produce millions of new white blood cells this week are also the cause of my fatigue and lack of immune defenses.

Germs are my enemy now, and the doctor and nurses have convinced me that I need to be more careful than ever. But I have my own bodyguard: Officer HHO. Bless his heart, he is taking his protective role very seriously.

But really, I wouldn't make it without him. As he said this morning, "We've been stuck together with super-strong velcro since February 9." Can you believe it hasn't even been two full months yet? Seems much longer.

While I am seriously grateful I haven't had the typical nausea and diarrhea side effects, I've had some 'other' minor ones. Gastro issues, predicted sensitivity to cold in my hands and mouth (touching anything cold feels like I'm being shocked), and sores in my mouth. The nurse gave me a special mouthwash this morning - hope it works!

I'm also trying to figure out what I have been eating that might be causing my gastro fits. This "process of elimination" seems to be just plain trial and error... patience, patience.

The 'new me' notices every little detail in more vivid color and 3D. I have been overwhelmed with the beautiful array of colorful wild flowers everywhere. I don't think the bluebonnets have ever been fuller or more vibrant. And I know I've never appreciated them sooo much! Enjoy!

xoxoxo, Karen

"While I was on chemo
I found it best if I stayed with a more bland diet ...
I also still avoid crowds and folks who insist upon kissing,
which I am sure you also do."
Jeanne C

"Emotional weekend.
Sending positive juju your way, Momma Owen.
We LOVE you and are inspired by your attitude and strength!
Keep up the good work!"
Jenny B

IT'S SATURDAY ALREADY
nupagen shots required

> "All this sounds great!
> So happy you and H
> got your dancing shoes out!
> XOXO"
> Kathy

April 7, 2018

No, I didn't skip town. In fact, quite the opposite. I finished another week of daily nupagen shots so that I can engage in another Triple C (remember: Chemo Crushes Cancer) day on Monday.

I am so thankful I am still feeling 'whole and healed.' In fact, those are the words I use to thank God for being with me on this journey every day.

I have felt so good that Howard and I donned our 'casual chic' attire and joined so many friends at the spring dance of our Dance Club last night. I'm talking about THE Austin Dance Club, which is the only Dance Club in Austin in existence since World War II.

Truth be told, we don't dance nearly as well as those post-World War II couples did, but I do have fun (Howard dances under duress). Today I am really tired (nap time) but good; however old man Owen has been complaining about his knees all day - really?

Fortunately for HHO, the next dance isn't until Halloween - and I fully intend to be there in costume. When my dear friend Judy (who is a miracle leukemia survivor as well as my role model) heard I had been out dancing, she called and said, "I name you Karen Strong! I can't believe you were out dancing."

So from this day forward, I am *Karen Strong*. I am also so appreciative of all my wonderful, supportive friends who were there last night cheering me on. Howard finally made me come home when the sweat started dripping from under my wig.

Because I'm finding my wig to be hot, and we all know how hot it gets during the Texas summer, I bought a short wig this week. I came home wearing it, and much to my surprise, Howard said he really liked it.

About 35 years ago, I cut my hair short and when Howard saw it, he said, "If I had wanted to marry someone with short hair, I would have." His approval proves anyone can change over time. (-:

We had to change our MD Anderson appointment to end of May. They want me to get more consistent chemo infusions before I do the 'restage' in Houston. BUT, the good news, if all goes well, I'll be able to go to Camp Owen Colorado this summer and take my chemo at the cancer center in Montrose, CO, under the direction of my Austin oncologist.

Please keep the prayers coming for good results at MD Anderson so I can go to CO this summer!

I hope you can tell I'm working hard to adapt to my 'new normal.' The key words here are 'working hard,' but as long as I'm feeling this good, hard work isn't an issue.

We're off for a quick walk and then dinner, but I'll let you know how Triple C Day goes Monday. Enjoy the weekend.

Luv ya, Karen Strong

"Ms Karen Strong!!
You are a rock star and a dance star!"
Jane B

TRIPLE C DAY #4
6 hours, 5 bags

"I am captivated by your courage, humor, and amazing attitude!
I expected nothing less... it was all of these things that made me
want to spend my last couple of years at IBM on your team!"
Diane Hower

April 9, 2018

All is well today - Howard and I tromped into the infusion room with all my bags of 'stuff I need for a chemo day', e.g., prayer shawl (it is always cold in here), computer, books, ear buds, phone, water bottle, snacks, back pillow, socks, notebook, eye mask, Kindle, +++.

My blood work was all GOOD, my oncologist is very pleased, I'm feeling good - so I'm all hooked up and getting my six-hour dose of 'life juice.' Howard, my soulmate, is by my side (remember, we're velcro buddies) for the duration - an amazing gift to be so loved.

I just looked up at my IV pole - and oh, the cocktails I'm getting. Five bags of liquid dripping into my port and through my body. Six hours worth of cocktails designed to keep me going.

Pretty scary and yet remarkable at the same time. Please keep the prayers coming that all this is actually working. I won't know until I go to MD Anderson at the end of May.

The next few days should be pretty boring (I hope), so you may not hear from me until the end of the week.

This stuff makes me sooo sleepy - so off to zzzzzz land.

Love, Karen Strong

"Keep dancing!! Love it! Rock on #Karenstrong!"
Rachel K

WHO PULLED MY PLUG?
too much ZZZZZZ time

> "Dear 'Karen Tired' - you are an amazing, inspiring strong woman,
> who is wise enough to share your feelings and your humanity."
> Lynn T

April 12, 2018

My chemo infusions Monday through Wednesday went fine, so I anticipated sailing through this cycle as I have the last two. When you least expect it, you get this whammy.

Gastro issues hit me in the dark of night and then when I couldn't go back to sleep, I was overwhelmed and consumed with the grief of losing Blake, which always leads to the complicated sadness tied to Averie. Sometimes, the tremendous pain my family has suffered over the last four years and the toll my prognosis is taking on them leaves me bereft. I just can't stem the tide of uncontrollable sorrow and loss.

I've been pushing hard to make progress and heal, but today the ugly force of chemo fatigue has drained me of all energy - and Howard has taken my phone and put me to bed - literally. I need to 'listen' to my body more intently because today I can hardly move and now realize I've been straining too hard.

My therapist says I need to learn to 'just be' - which is very contrary to my nature. I still haven't mastered this mind-space.

But this is going to be a great weekend. Scott is flying in from Fayetteville, AR, by himself (left Liz and my grandbabies behind) to spend the weekend with me and Howard. Our wonderful son said he wanted a weekend by himself just to be able to spend time with me. I will have him to myself until Sunday afternoon - what a gift for any mother!

And of course, the other kids will be coming by to see Scott, so I may get to see everyone this weekend. Going to try to get some zzzz's before Scott gets here.

Karen Strong is on hiatus today.
Have a great weekend.

Love, Karen Tired

"You may be 'Karen Tired' but you are always 'Karen Loved'."
Jane B

"The beauty of life is that you can be whoever you want to be
and on whatever day you choose.
You were never in a Indian Guide Princess Tribe,
so it's time for your tribal name of the day.
I name you 'Brave Karen' today!
Love you."
Patti B

Best Bluebonnets Ever
Scott: What a son!

"What an awesome night it was!
Thank you for hosting us.
Friends forever."
Cameron S

April 17, 2018

Spring has sprung in TX and we have the most abundant and beautiful bluebonnets and wildflowers everywhere. What a poignant symbol of rebirth and growth! And least that's the way I'm taking it all in.

How often does a mother have three days with her adult son? We had the most wonderful time with Scott last weekend - from boating to walking the hike and bike trails, attending the Colin's Hope Gala, to great restaurants and the opportunity to have uninterrupted discussions, telling funny stories from Scott's teen years, etc., etc. Such a gift that he has overcome so much to become such a wonderful man - father, husband, son... a weekend for my memory books.

Then last night I had another amazing experience. My wonderful partner, Cam, from IBM, scheduled a class in Austin this week, and my colleague John blessed us with his amazing culinary skills and prepared a 5-star gourmet meal for me, Howard, Cam, Pam, Carl, Rachel, and Jane (Jane was on my team many moons ago and we have stayed friends for 15 years. It was such an honor that she came in just to see me!).

It was so amazing that all these dear IBMers came to visit me, but to have them here for such a wonderful meal was icing on the cake (in fact, dessert was chocolate cake from my baker-friend extraordinaire, Miz P). I love these guys and have missed them all terribly.

It was a magical evening outside on the patio with funny stories, cherished companionship, and course after course of John's delectable offerings. It doesn't get any better... and tomorrow night, we're hosting this team as well as the sales exec coaches who are coming in to participate in the session this week.

Another reconnect with special IBMers. I am thriving on this love and support... and am so excited to have the extended teach/coaching team for dinner tomorrow night. I really miss my job, so seeing my colleagues is extra special.

Yesterday (Monday), I had my first of this week's daily nupagen shots. Time to build up my blood cell count again. I'm feeling fatigued because it is quite a strain to build white blood cells from 0.7 to 10,000 (somethings) every other week. But that's the task for the week - so I'm 'on it'.

I've also confirmed my MD Anderson appointment in Houston for May 15-17. Big days ahead!

Today is the seven-month anniversary of Blake's passing. Jan (my dear friend and Blake's godmother) and I spent some time at his and Averie's graves today. (They are next to each other.)

I'm not capable of describing the depth and breadth of complex emotions wrought by missing him so much while trying to take one day at a time during my intense healing journey. But I do believe Blake is at my side and supporting me during this journey.

With that belief, *Karen Strong* is back!

Enjoying the beautiful spring weather,
Karen Strong

"I am amazed by your strength, Mom!
You are and always have been an inspiration.
Thank you for the amazing weekend and the life you have given me.
I love you with all my heart!"
Scott O

photo by *Twinty Photography*

A 'New Normal' Week in Review
doctors, doctors, and more doctors

> "I've loved your inspiring writings for years
> but never as much as now.
> You are amazing. Yea for you!"
> Susan R

April 22, 2018

When I wrote last Tuesday, I was anticipating my second IBM dinner of the week on Wednesday night. It couldn't have been better (other than two colleagues got sick and couldn't attend): another beautiful night outside with such amazing and interesting colleagues.

As always, we got so caught up in our IBM-speak (acronyms, acronyms, acronyms), Howard finally slipped into the house and did the dishes. But what a wonderful, memorable evening. Thank you, Cam (Toronto), John (New Jersey), Steve (Virginia), Stacy (Dallas), Sadi (Toronto), Pam (Boston), Michelle (Las Vegas), Carl (Atlanta), Rachel (Chicago).

I did spend every morning at the doctor's office, getting my shots this week, and I did have some side effects - back pain and gastro issues again. But not to be deterred, I continued with my meditation, sound therapy, and even went to my first Singing Bowls session.

Singing bowls, you might ask? Suggest you look it up on Google for a better explanation than I could give. But what an effective ancient form of meditation therapy - so totally relaxing and balancing my shakras.

I also learned that I need more sleep/rest this week, so I took naps, responded to emails, texts, and focused on rest and healing. Then Saturday night (after resting Saturday), we attended friend Bob's 65th birthday where I saw so many of my supporters and prayer warriors.

Again, it is so rejuvenating to be surrounded by such love and positive energy. Many of the friends at this party are parents of Blake's friends, so though it was very good, it was also awfully bad as the memories are once again so poignant and disrupting my sleep.

But the big news of the week: my brother Gary, founder and CEO of Phoenix Thera-laser Systems out of Dallas, drove to Austin with one of his super-duper laser machines. He brought a technician to begin my therapeutic laser treatments. These treatments have proven to reduce pain and help rebuild depleted immune systems, e.g., rebuilding white and red blood cells.

As you know, my white cell counts have fluctuated wildly every time I have a chemo treatment. The counts drop to 0, and then I spend the non-chemo week getting shots to rebuild. This is very hard on anyone's body - which I experienced in spades this week.

What a 'just in time' blessing. Howard, friend Jan, sons Jeffrey and Steven, and daughter Tiffany all came over this afternoon to learn how to administer these laser treatments if we don't have a technician available. Quite an afternoon! And Gary thinks he may have his first Austin location open by September.

Tomorrow, Howard's brother Mark and his wife Betsy are flying in from Ohio for the week to see me/us. They have been so supportive of us the last 4½ years through all our travails. We are so excited to see them.

Tomorrow is a Triple-C day, the beginning of another 2-week cycle. Getting geared up for 6 hours of infusions followed by the external pump of ongoing chemo-cocktails until Wednesday is a pretty tall order, but I'm up to it! This will be Triple-C day #5 - and the goal is to get through 7 so I can go to MD Anderson.

Onward with love and appreciation,
Karen Strong

Additional trivia: It has been a standing joke among family and friends for about two years that Howard and Karen have the saggiest old bed in the area (looks like a 'w' with a big hump in the middle). Yet Howard has insisted it is just fine - after all, it is only 16 years old. Well, wonders never cease and we are having a new bed delivered tomorrow. I'm hoping for No More Back Pain! Fingers crossed. Good nite all...

"It's great to see you appreciating the small and the big things.
I love your positive attitude and your strength.
xoxo"
Bonnie D

GOOD NEWS WEDNESDAY
Laser treatments designed for *successful* healing

"Yoga is so much more than exercise! It also incorporates
some of the energy and vibrational work you refer to.
Sending you my energy through positive thoughts!"
Beatriz F

April 25, 2018

Just returned from the doctor's office with good news. Today is the last day of my Triple-C #5 chemo treatment when they remove the external pump. I've shared that they do CBC blood work 3 times per week - so today was one of those days.

Before my first chemo treatment, of course, they did vast and broad testing. There are three liver tests that are critical to liver function. Two of those tests have always been relatively within limits for me, but the most important liver function test was really bad. A normal count for this test is 135 - and my liver count was 1985 (over 2000 can be liver failure).

And today, my count is down to 318 - amazing in 2½ months. I am so grateful and excited to believe I am whole and healing.

The other big measure of improvement I heard today is about my white blood cell count. For the past 6 weeks, at this point in my chemo cycle, my white cell count has gone down to 700 (should be around 10,000), so that's why all the nupagen shots. But today, my white cell count was only down to 3900, which is a big improvement.

Could this be a very fast response to the 1½ laser treatments I've had? If so, and if I keep improving, will that mean fewer or no nupagen shots? My brother Gary, who has provided his laser machine for me, feels I may actually be responding to laser this quickly - I sure hope so.

Stay tuned. Anyway, I'm on a mid-week high.

You all know I'm focused on a holistic approach to beating this cancer. I've shared that I'm doing chemo, meditation, sound therapy, Singing Bowls,

CBD-THC oil, vitamins and supplements, plant-based diet with only fish and chicken - everything organic, gluten-free and dairy-free (a tough dietary road, but doable when my risk factors are this high). But I haven't shared two additional alternative approaches I've taken.

I won't share one of one of them now because I haven't started it yet, and I don't know if it will have enough time to germinate by the time I do my next Pet Scan in Houston on May 15. So I'll save this unbelievable story with you after I discover my status at MD Anderson.

But my second outreach has been to see a Shaman (otherwise known as a healer). Jenifer studied, trained, and was certified in Peru. I have learned sooo much, and I truly believe that her cleansing and healing sessions have made a huge difference for me.

We have so much to learn about our universe, energy, ancient healing practices, etc., etc. I can tell when my brain and heart are in alignment, when she balances my shakras, when we focus on energy, because everything in the universe is energy.

And most important, a strong connection exists between ancient healers and Christianity. I never realized the two worlds would be so inter-related. Jenifer has been instrumental in helping me progress in my spiritual journey - and the value of approaching my transformation holistically. I am very open to everything new. And why not? I've learned so much more about the afterlife and Eastern and South American religious and healing practices. And it all makes so much sense and has been very helpful to me. I'm working on 'being in the moment', taking each day at a time.

We're having a great time with Mark and Betsy - and keeping super busy. More to come -

With love and such appreciation,
Karen Strong

"I've read this entry twice
because it makes me so happy!"
Kathy R

CHALLENGING SATURDAY
missing a special wedding

"A friend sent me:
'Grief is like the ocean;
it comes in waves, ebbing and flowing.
Sometimes the water is calm, and sometimes it is overwhelming.
All we can do is learn to swim.'
You're doing a very good job of swimming.
I love you."
Kathy G

April 28, 2018

It is a beautiful Saturday morning, and Howard just gave me my laser treatment. You have to know this is a serious commitment for Howard. He is not accustomed to exacting focus and patience, which is necessary for these treatments. But he did a GREAT job. Kudos HHO!

As I last reported, my numbers looked really good Wednesday and again Thursday, so my reward was NO nupagen shots last week. I'll go in Monday for more blood work and see if I'll need them next week.

Once I got my pump off Wednesday, I had significant chemo side effects and have had them for three days now. What a downer and a disappointing change from previous weeks. But as long as my numbers keep improving, I'll push through this hurdle.

Kyle Samouce (Blake's best friend and best man) and Kelly are getting married tonight. I love these kids and we were planning to attend the wedding, but as we've come closer and closer to their special day, I have had anxiety and emotional trauma. All of Blake's friends will be there. Blake was supposed to be in the wedding.

I just can't attend and see everyone who was at Blake's wedding and funeral. I'm sending love and best wishes to Kyle and Kelly, but staying home. My shattered heart just can't take any more wrenching grief today...

We're on our way to take a walk in this beautiful weather. I need to refocus on gratitude for this gorgeous day and have faith that God will provide the strength I need to take each days as it comes. God will bring me a sense of peace that Blake is where God wants him, and faith that Blake is also with me and helping me on this challenging journey.

Have a great weekend.
Karen Strong

"Know that God and Blake are always near.
May this week bring good things.
And, Howard, way to go!
Maybe a new Laser career ahead."
Judy W

"You are doing an AMAZING job of taking care of yourself!
I had to skip weddings, too. Just couldn't do it.
It's OK! Give yourself a 'pass'."
Kathy

ALL SYSTEMS GO
wildflowers and hummingbirds

"I love how you talk about Howard!
Y'all are truly the best of friends and SO in love.
It's beautiful!"
Jenny B Q

April 29, 2018

Beautiful Sunday morning. My bad side effects are gone, so feeling good! Looking forward to a great day, and then will get my blood checked in the morning.

Keeping fingers crossed that I won't need nupagen shots this week. In the interim, sitting here in my La-Z-Boy chair enjoying our wildflower garden and watching the hummingbirds and bees relish the nectar of this wild conglomeration.

Enjoy,
Karen Strong

"So glad you are feeling better!!
I can see you sitting there!
Please tell your hummingbirds
to stop by my new feeder. :-)"
Jane B

Cloudy Monday
drizzly, cloudy, overcast

"The sunshine will return,
and your white blood count cell will go up again.
Prayers, hugs, and lots of love for you!"
Alegria

April 30, 2018

My mood is like the weather today - drizzly, cloudy, overcast. I went to the doctor this morning, and didn't expect to discover that after my good numbers last week, my white blood cell count has bottomed out again.

So nupagen shots every morning this week to build up for chemo next Monday. Gotta do what I gotta do!

Pushing forward,
Karen Strong

"So sorry your mood is like the weather.
This will sound so corny: weather will
clear and you will feel the warmth of the sun,
as will the shots help you."
Lynn T

WEDNESDAY HAS BURST
AMONG US
wearing an ankle bracelet

"Hang in there, friend …
you are a rock star."
Bonnie D

May 2, 2018

Next week will be three months since I was diagnosed. Sometimes it seems like three months, and other days it seems like three years. I sort of feel like I'm wearing a prisoner's ankle bracelet because I can't leave town. Very confining feeling for someone who has spent her last 10 years traveling for both professional (the majority) and personal purposes.

When I think about it, February 9th marked the beginning of a new chapter in my life. And what a chapter it has become. I am refocusing on taking one day at a time, being grateful every day, and maximizing this journey to the unknown.

It is definitely easier to refocus when I'm feeling better, and the good news is, I *am* feeling better. The derailing chemo effects of the past week have now disappeared. Believe me, I am MOST grateful for feeling good (though still tired) again. Moving forward with daily shots toward Monday's next round of chemo.

I have spent my entire life trying to LOSE weight. Over the years, I have been on every diet known to woman and have yo-yo'ed with the best of them, including Oprah!

So with crooked smile and tongue in cheek, I hear I should NOT lose weight, and am intrigued that I have no appetite, don't want to eat, find everything tasteless or like metal, and am not focused on weight but on eating what I need to keep up my strength and blood counts. I've lost 33 lbs and—surprise!—I can wear ALL the clothes in my closet. In fact, I'm now culling items that are TOO big. Holy cow, what a new experience.

Another 10-15 pounds, and I will have to go shopping for smaller sizes…

with mixed feelings. But for the time being, I am pulling on clothes I didn't even remember keeping. And now I'm glad I did.

I wouldn't recommend this approach to dieting for anyone, but there definitely is a silver lining. I'm still around and doing well enough to 'look my best' under the circumstances.

Blood work tomorrow. Please keep the prayers coming for good blood counts. I figure God can't ignore all the prayers coming His way on my behalf. I don't mind if the greasiest wheel gets greased! Thanks all!

Keeping on keeping on,
Karen Strong

"I believe in miracles! Big prayers for you always.
So glad you are feeling good.
Keep that spirit because positive attitudes win battles!
Hugs!"
Belinda K

TRIPLE C DAY #6
my poison cocktail

"This is Austin telling Houston to get ready.
KO is on her way!!!
MDA has no idea what they are in store for.
Give em %#*!!
Well... maybe not that strong.
However, they will catch on quickly."
Sandy P

May 7, 2018

A beautiful clear-blue-sky Monday projected to reach 92° - awesome! I'm at the Infusion lab getting my bi-weekly life-restoring poison cocktail, and glad to be here because getting chemo means I can keep my appointment at MD Anderson next week! Onward!

We've been focusing on that appointment and are ready to conquer. We'll be there from Tuesday - Thursday. Please keep the prayers coming for good reports from Houston next Thursday.

As you know, the last ten days have been wrought with gastro issues. I was so scared I was regressing. When I saw my oncologist this morning, he didn't feel like my challenges were tied to my chemo, but that I had probably caught something from someone who was sick - sigh!

So I'm going to get more serious about not exposing myself to those nasty germs out there in the big bad world: more caution during my low immunity days.

And I also had some regression on my blood counts. When I came in this morning, my white blood cell count was really down low—which hasn't ever happened on a chemo day—so I'm grateful they gave me chemo anyway.

My doctor also said my liver is having trouble absorbing fats, so if I have any more gastro issues, he'll prescribe a new med I will have to take with every meal.

But that's okay. I'm confident this week will be a good one. How can it not be, with all this wonderful sunshine and blue skies? What could be better than going home this afternoon and absorbing some D3 rays? Maybe I'll even pull out my Brazilian bikini from our days on the beaches of Ipanema and Copacabana - hah, good thing our pool is so private! (-: My kids are cringing right now, but that would certainly make Howard LOL.

Yesterday, we celebrated our granddaughter Westyn's 6th birthday at our house. The party brought back many memories of the years and years of swim parties we had for our 5 kids, and I love doing this (upon request) for our grandkids.

It was just an old fashioned backyard party: pizza, fruit, chips and salsa, cake and ice cream to feed those always-hungry little tummies. And swimming, putt-putt, badminton, soccer (I put out the goals), bean bag toss, basketball, and a piñata to expend all that sugar-high energy!

Happiness is watching our outgoing red-headed Westyn be a social butterfly *extraordinaire* with all her cousins and friends. I will admit Howard and I were exhausted last evening, something I don't remember back when we were in our 30's and 40's.

Sleepy time now from all these drugs. So until... zzzzzzz.

> With so much appreciation and love,
> Karen Strong

> "It sounds like you had a fantastic party.
> What great memories.
> Praying for blessings."
> Anna S

T.G.I.F.
enjoying my backyard zen-like garden

May 10, 2018

It has been a pretty good week, chemo Monday thru Wednesday, nupagen shot Thursday. Nothing today because my white cell count was high (Good surprise!) - so a four-day hiatus until next Tuesday at MD Anderson.

Thanks to so many of you who have sent good wishes, prayers, cards, texts, messages; I feel like we're taking an army of support to Houston next week. And I am sooo confident we'll have good news to report by Thursday evening! I am already happy to report that my liver enzymes improved again this week - remember when I started, my liver enzyme count was a high and dangerous 1985? This week, the enzyme count is 245 - great improvement (130 is normal).

It has been a glorious week of sunshine and great weather in bustling Austin, TX. And I've spent stress-free and peaceful time this week reading, relaxing and meditating in our backyard Zen-like garden while enjoying the cool water of the pool. We've also spent wonderful, relaxing time out on our boat *Nirvana*. Great prep for all the upcoming lab work and scans coming Tuesday.

Happy Mother's Day to all! While I'm looking forward to being with family for Mother's Day Sunday, this will also be another first without our Blake. Every 'first' is so emotional and tough. If only...

Thanks to ALL for your love, prayers, and support,
Karen Strong

My First MD Anderson Experience
jaw-dropping

Sending love and hugs to you and Howard. So glad you are in with one of
the best medical teams in the world! Keeping you in my daily prayers."
Marlene H

May 16, 2018

Thank you, Fran, for your Facebook update—and to all of you who have
commented and sent your love, prayers and support for my recovery—and for
my long awaited appointment at MD Anderson Cancer Center in Houston.

It seems as though we've been waiting months and months for this week
to arrive. But here we are and what an experience!

This entire MDA medical complex is beyond comprehension, an amazing
city unto itself. With 20,000 employees at MDA Houston (every one of them
well-trained, friendly, and kind), the entire megaplex is run with Army
precision. Needless to say, it is huge, yet pleasing, colorful and spotless.

We stayed at the affiliated Rotary House International (a Marriott) that
is connected to the med center by an overhead walkway. Today, we had to be
in four different locations, so we tested the effectiveness of their directions –
and found our locations with relative ease.

And it is amazing that MDA is just one of the many hospital complexes
in this well-planned megaplex medical community in Houston. I don't think
another vast set of medical facilities in one organized area of a city exists
anywhere else in the world. Do you know of any others?

What did we do and learn? We had four separate appointments.
1) Registration – even though I had pre-registered
2) Appointment with Dr. Javle (world-renowned pancreatic oncologist),
   + through my brother Gary's MD business consultant, I was able to
   see Dr. Paul White
3) Blood work
4) CT Scan

And since we won't have the results until Thursday when we see Dr. Javle again, we're heading home tonight and we'll drive back to Houston early Thursday morning. Better to sleep in our own bed than toss and turn in the hotel for the next two nights.

What did we find out today in our meeting with Dr. Javle? Guarded optimism until we get test results back Thursday. He said, "You look great. Are you getting ready for a cruise? Are you sure you're sick?"

I had to give him the evil eye...

He smiled and said my blood work from last week in Austin looked good, my alkaloid phosphate (???) liver enzymes had improved dramatically since early February, and it is amazing that I still have no pain. He gave me an unexpected COLOR (brand) test for hereditary cancer, in hopes he can identify a genetic marker to my pancreatic cancer. As a result of this test, I'll be able to tell my family, siblings, kids, and cousins if they are predisposed.

The serious issue he addressed is my ongoing (TMI?) diarrhea. He said it is the lack of my pancreas' ability to produce the enzymes necessary to digest my food. So he gave me an RX for pancreatic enzymes to take with each meal as well as a new Anti-D RX. Here's hoping for a new me within a few days. And, of course, I'll get all test results when we return to Houston early Thursday morning.

It was a very long day, and I am exhausted. I had great intentions to continue my research during my wait periods, but the day was so busy, I reverted to reading my anti-stress mystery book (You might like it: *Saving Sophie* by Ronald Balson - lightweight and entertaining).

Surprise, surprise; Howard talked to people from all over the world - Saudi Arabia, Chile, Oregon, Kentucky, Florida, Europe, +++. And the common factor across the world? MD Anderson in the mecca of hope and healing for all types of cancer. I am now a convert, too. I told Dr. Javle I came to him specifically to apply his expertise and broad knowledge base to extending my life. He said, "That's the plan!"

When we go back on Thursday, I'll have many questions for him, one of which will be, "Given my current test results, what is my life expectancy now?" I'm sure he will say more than eleven months - especially since I told him I wanted ten years. I'll be writing to you Thursday night to give you all the news - which I hope will be nothing but good.

Prayers and fingers crossed for the next few days. Until Thursday night,
Karen Strong

"Sounds like Dr. Javle is the man! You are fortunate to be under his care."
Sandy P

And The Doctor Said,
"Very, very good results!"
33% reduction welcome

"Thinking of you as we sit here...
P.S. I am taking credit that your alkaloid phosphate liver enzymes
had improvement by my cooking the dinner at your house."
John D

May 17, 2018

Howard and I are overjoyed and so grateful for the wonderful news we received today at MD Anderson. First, Dr. Javle's assistant walked in and said, "Very, very good results" She then proceeded to show us my first CT scan (three months ago) vs. Tuesday's CT scan.

Amazing! Of the eleven tumors in my liver, the smallest ones have disappeared and the larger ones have shrunk an average of 39%. Then she showed me that my pancreatic tumor has shrunk 33%.

Just Tuesday, Dr. Javle (pancreatic oncologist) told me pancreatic tumors don't shrink; they just help or hinder pancreatic function. And I've been having bad gastro issues because my pancreas is not producing enzymes.

But when Dr. Javle walked in today, he smiled and said, "I lied; I told you pancreatic tumors don't shrink; but your pancreatic tumor has shrunk 33% - which is rare."

Then he told me to continue my chemo and whatever else I'm doing (so many alternative approaches I've shared over the last few months) and to return to MDA in two months, when we'll repeat all the tests and choose next steps.

I'm surprised he wants to see me in two months, because the usual time span is three-four months. Now I'm doubling down on everything good (including my restricted and boring diet), continuing with my bi-weekly Monday/Wednesday chemo treatments, and hoping y'all will continue to pray for my total recovery.

I'm certainly not out of the woods, and Dr. Javle said every series of tests determines ongoing treatment, recovery and longevity. He is collaborating with my Austin oncologist to tweak a few ingredients of my chemo cocktail. With the great news today, I'm pumped for chemo Monday, now I know it is working.

Today is May 17, the eight-month anniversary of Blake's death, another difficult day full of grief and loss, but also many touching memories. Howard, my kids, my extended family, and many friends believe Blake has had a lot to do with my remarkable results today.

I believe that, too. I know he is with me. I know he sits next to me at chemo treatments, and if I know my Blaker, he has been using his amazing communications skills to secure God's support for me. Besides, Howard says Blake isn't ready for me to impede his heavenly freedom just yet. Blake is probably telling God I need more time on this earth to accomplish my new goals and projects.

I am so grateful for today, for my results, and for all YOUR prayers and support, and so much more. I love your 'Hearts' and 'Comments' on Caring Bridge and on Facebook. You keep me going. But please, your work is not done - I still need your prayers and am counting on you. Help me to stay 'Karen Strong' on my challenging journey.

xoxoxo, K

"You deserve that wonderful news!
You have worked so hard to do everything
you can to fight this cancer.
Blake has been with you every minute of every day,
helping you. We will continue our prayers."
Betsy and Mark

Back To Reality: 3C
chemo crushes cancer
#8 delayed
gastric issues rule

"Naps are to be embraced!!!!!"
Martha V

May 22, 2018

I shouldn't be disappointed after my great news last week, but it was still hard to hear that I couldn't get my chemo infusion yesterday. Even more than usual, my white blood cell count was at rock bottom (back to nupagen shots every day this week). My gastro issues have totally depleted me - so much so that I am now on 2 antibiotics and will receive an anti-diarrheal shot tomorrow that is supposed to eliminate the problem for an entire month! Yikes - I am a little apprehensive but also excited for some relief. Now in build-up mode to be able to do my chemo next Tuesday.

Yesterday morning, we reviewed my MDA reports with my Austin oncologist and he couldn't have been more pleased with my CT results. He said I am doing better than 98% of his patients; my chemo nurse said, "Amazing!" I am holding on dearly to these sincere and extemporaneous responses from every medical person I run into. I've already set up my next MDA visit for July 30-31, and we'll run through the same tests and CT scan again. I have high expectations for continued success.

And the best news yet: We can go to CO this summer! Dr. Shimkus (my Austin oncologist) has sent a referral/request for coordination with San Juan Cancer Center in Montrose, CO, for them to be able to treat me under Dr. Shimkus' direction.

Fingers crossed they will accept me as a summer patient. I totally expect to be 'accepted' because they said they have this same situation with many Texans each summer, and I have good insurance. (Chemo treatments are the gravy trains for oncologists.)

The plan today is to leave around June 13 and return to Austin the third week of July. We'll stay here for 1~2 weeks, head to Houston, and then fly back to CO around Aug 4 until early October.

I am extra excited that Liz drove to Austin from AR yesterday with my beautiful grandchildren, Carson (3) and Amelia (15 months). It is quite a drive with children that age. She left at 9 AM and arrived at our doorstep at 6 PM. I hadn't seen them since February, and you know how much they grow and change every day at these ages.

We will 'play' all week, and then Scott will fly in Friday night for the Memorial Day weekend. And all the kids and grandkids will come over Sunday to see Scott, Liz, and the kids before they have to drive back on Monday. I just hate that they are so far away.

Another side-effect of my deficiency is fatigue. I am now taking naps most days. THIS is a big change for me. But I am counting on feeling much better by next week, so all is well.

Have a wonderful Memorial Day weekend. Enjoy every minute with your loved ones.

xoxo,
Karen Strong

"Naps? You are complaining about naps? Really?
Naps rock (just like you!). Embrace the almighty nap.
In fact, according to a very reliable source (me), napping in Colorado
in the summer is the MOST therapeutic thing you can do.
Congrats on your amazing progress!!
We all cheered last week when Cam told us about your results!!"
Carl McI

Back On Track: 3C
chemo crushes cancer
#8 in progress right now!
grandkids rule

"Woohoo. As the sign in my bar says,
'You call it CHAOS... we call it FAMILY'.
Love you!"
Patty B

May 29, 2018

I hope y'all (very Texan) had as terrific a Memorial Day weekend as I did. Great fun with the kids and grandkids boating, swimming, movies, walking, playing - and in my case, watching the grandkids bond and make new family memories.

Liam (Steven's 3-year-old) and Carson (Scott's 3-year-old) became best buddies this weekend, and all our hearts melted when they hugged and told each other they loved each other (totally unassisted). It was almost heart-breaking when they had a long, drawn out goodbye last night. (Scott, Liz, Carson and Amelia are on their way back to Fayetteville today.)

Having Carson and Amelia here all last week was a fabulous therapeutic 'connect with Nana' week, and little Miss Amelia (15 months) cried when I left for chemo this morning, and my all-boy Carson told me he would miss me. That coming from my 3-year-old 'pistol.'

Though I'm exhausted from all the activity, I wouldn't trade even one minute of all the family fun, and now I'm sitting here getting chemo for 6 hours - so a time to stay still and nap!

Last week was a typical gyroscope between gastro issues and nausea, but part of these bothersome issues must be tied to the two antibiotics I'm on to prevent sepsis. Man, that scared me, but I believe the threat is behind me. Today is the last day for these antibiotics and I'm looking forward to reduced nausea. I just found out that the doctor reduced the concentration of my chemo cocktail by 33% because of my intolerance to the dose I was getting.

I have to survive the chemo to fight the cancer, so it's a good thing I trust my doctor. I'm focusing on taking it one day at a time and maximizing each day (not easy to do!).

This Friday our newest grandson (Ford Ellis Owen) will arrive to Jeff and Lisa via C-section. We can't wait! This is our miracle baby, who was conceived the night of Blake's death. And, via ultrasound, we've learned he already has a full head of spiky hair, just like Blake when he was born. We don't think it will be black hair like Blake's, as all of Jeff's family has blond hair. We can't wait to meet Ford!

I know it seems as though a lot of what I write doesn't have much to do with my cancer, but it really does. Being with family, though missing Blake and Averie terribly, is the reason I'm working so hard to stay alive. If we can classify all the fun and chaos of the Owen family as 'therapy,' then I have the best therapy in the world. And I have all of YOU to share it with. Thank you for being my extended family!

> With love and appreciation,
> Karen Strong

P.S. Howard is really digging the new me, with a great tan and -40 lbs. since February. Though I don't get in the sun, I'm getting rays from the reflection off the lake water and in the pool. I'm still not interested in food. Now I'm focused on not losing more, but when nothing looks, tastes, or smells good, what's the point?

> "I miss you!!! It's been too long!
> I need some Mama Karen in my life.
> Wanna hear from the horse's mouth what's up!
> Coffee, walk the trail, you name it. Love you, Mom.
> You're absolutely CRUSHING IT!
> So proud. #karenstrong!!"
> Jenny B Q

MOTHERS WILL TOTALLY 'GET IT'
déja vu of pregnancy days

"Oh boy, do I remember the nausea preggo days!
I couldn't leave dishes in the sink because
the smell would get me every time!
You are right though, preggo hardship does lead to
bringing home beautiful babies...
your prize at the end of this hardship
will be kicking some cancer ass!!!
Love you, my friend! Keep on winning!"
Rachel K

May 30, 2018

Back in March/April I was flying through my chemo with few side effects and thinking, "Not such a bad deal after all." I also remember one of the oncology nurses warning me about the cumulative side effects of ongoing chemo. Well, May has been my month of reckoning.

After my A-D shot last week, I've seen a big improvement on that end (*double entendre*). However, I'm brought back to my many years of being pregnant (six times) with so many months of nausea.

Fellow Moms, I'm sure you can remember just the smell or sight of food would send you into gags and sweats. Or the feeling of that massive lump in your throat, just like the bottle cork that won't move. And yes, I am taking nausea meds when it gets too bad, but I don't like the sleepiness of phenargren. I'm thinking back to those long-ago PG months when the result was a beautiful and precious baby. Now I'm hoping the result will be continued tumor shrinkage and therefore longer life.

My very professional and non-emotional Austin oncologist did at last say he thought I would make it at least two years, which is a far cry from my original prognosis of from two to eleven months. But my goal is still six+ years, so please keep those prayers and support coming my way. I know THIS takes a village and strong prayer warriors.

I'm waiting to hear if the San Juan Cancer Center will accept me as a summer patient so we can go to CO. Should know by tomorrow - fingers crossed. But I have confirmed they will take my insurance. Whew!

Working this cancer gig is a full-time job. Been on the phone all morning sorting things out, now off to complete more forms... There are so many stacks of stuff on my desk, I can't find anything; sometime in the near future I guess I'll have to get organized once again.

Can't believe how hot it is already - really need to get to CO but have been told they are also having higher temps than ever. Who says there isn't global warming?

Hanging in,
Karen Strong

"This journal reminded me of you and that time
I got tacos when you were pregnant!
It was so bad that you walked around Dollar General
and still made me eat outside of the car!"
Mollie C

JUNE 1 - A GLORIOUS DAY TO REMEMBER
11th grandchild arrives

"Good news, Karen Strong!
Do I need to refer to you as 'KS' versus 'KO'?
Not sure I can make the change. :)
xoxoxoxoxo"
Bonnie D

June 1, 2018

Ford Ellis Owen, our 11th grandchild, was born at 2:15 PM today, weighing in at 7 lbs. 11 oz. (just like his daddy, Jeff) and 19 3/8 inches long.

He is adorable with a head of light brown hair and a cute little dimple in his chin just like Lisa's. We are so grateful that everyone is doing so well. We've just brought big sisters Laney and Riley home with us to spend the night before we return tomorrow for more baby Ford bonding.

Another reason this day is so enjoyable: for the first time in about five weeks, I feel great.

No nausea, D, or fatigue. What a glorious day to remember.

xo, Karen Strong

"Wow, Karen! A date to remember for sure!!
Congratulations to you and Howard for your newest arrival.
How sweet that your grandchildren spent the nite with y'all."
Cookie B

LEARNING NEW LESSONS
EVERY WEEK!
my own fault

"You are a shining light to all of us, Karen...
keep up the good work and
we out here in cyber space will keep up the prayers."
Marion M

June 6, 2018

It's all my fault. Shame on me.

Lisa warned me that Riley had a cold and sore throat last weekend while Laney and Riley were coming to stay with us. And I said, "I really want the girls to stay with us anyway - and I'll just not get too close."

Well, I've now learned my lesson because I have the cold and sore throat, I'm back on a Z-pack, but I think the cold is viral, which make the Z-pack proactive so I don't get another bacterial infection. I now know I need to be more careful and stay away from those kid germs - though NOT seeing my grandkids is really tough. But even worse, I can't hold Ford now, so I'm determined to be well in 48 hours... must have a daily goal and focus!

Good news: We're approved for chemo treatments at the San Juan Cancer Center in CO! They will collaborate with my oncologist here, so I'll have great care up there, too. We're flying to Camp Owen CO on Thursday, June 14, and returning to Austin July 25.

While we're there, Howard and I will have a week to open the house and get ready for the summer. Then Steven, Shannon, Westyn, Liam, and Brazos will be with us for two weeks followed by Jeff, Lisa, Laney, Riley, and baby Ford. We are so excited to get up in the cool mountain air in our very special piece of heaven. (And where it is not 98-100 degrees every day.)

I was also approved for long-term disability today - a very good thing! Really relieves the stress level and will allow me to continue my intense recovery journey with the time to meet all the demands of being a cancer patient.

I must say, IBM has been a Godsend. And my IBM colleagues are also amazing and continue to reach out to me with so much love and support.

My new normal is accepting each day as a cancer patient with the associated focus on whatever pops up that day, e.g., I just started feeling better, having overcome the D and nausea, and here I am with a cold and sore throat.

Big deal? Not for the old Karen, but a big deal for Karen Strong.

I'm now in my fifth month of treatments, and OH! the lessons I've learned. I'm getting another undergraduate degree in Cancer, though I can think of better majors.

FYI: I read EACH comment every single one of you sends. I view the 'hearts' each day. I also review texts, emails, cards, and VMs. I appreciate every point of contact from each of you.

I hope you understand that I can't possibly reach out to each of you every day. There just are not enough hours in the day. But your messages, words, and prayers sustain me. Thank you, thank you, thank you! And keep 'em coming.

Living my new normal,
Karen Strong

"My nurse friend calls little children 'Petri dishes.'
Whenever my grands are sick, Nana brings home a souvenir.
Especially bad for you, I know!
Those cuddles are usually worth it!
Love you and I think of you every day."
Susan R

IT'S MY BIRTHDAY!
69 and counting

"Happy Birthday! Chilling on the boat
and in the pool sounds like a worthwhile goal.
Looking forward to your 70th!
Prayers and blessings!"
Anna S

June 11, 2018

The old Karen never would have publicized another birthday. The new Karen is shouting from the rooftops that today is my 69th birthday.

Surprised I would share this closely guarded secret? (A woman never tells her age.) I'm even surprised at myself.

But, as you know, everything has changed since the beginning of February. I'll never forget the doctor telling Howard, me, Jeffrey, and Steven that I could have as little as three weeks to live. I remember turning to my 'men' and assuring them I would be here for Ford's (Jeff's new son) birth, which I witnessed on June 1 and for my birthday.

At that time, I had no idea if I would in fact be here, and I am so grateful to be celebrating and feeling so good: I am feeling recovered. Last week was tough with a cold, sore throat and more antibiotics, but I have been really feeling healthy since Saturday.

And today on my blue ribbon birthday, I have had so many texts, calls, messages, cards, and gifts, I am overwhelmed with joy, love and gratitude. Thank you ALL!

At dinner tonight, Howard and I decided we're going to throw a 70th birthday bash next year. I am committed to continuing my multifaceted healing journey with God as my co-pilot. I KNOW God cannot ignore all the prayers coming his way on my behalf.

Today didn't start out so well. I arrived at the cancer center for my bi-weekly chemo infusion. The first procedure is to draw my blood to see if there is anything out of whack. And wouldn't you know it, my blood count was again way down in the basement

No chemo this week, a return to daily nupagen shots, and chemo rescheduled for next week - which means no trip to CO this Thursday. So disappointing.

You may have heard about the huge forest fires in Durango burning out of control, and the high winds blowing the smoke over the mountains into our Ridgway/Telluride area. Smoke-filled air is so pervasive around our house that there is near-zero visibility and pulmonary issues for anyone with medical concerns. I cannot go up there until the air is clear, which is not projected to happen until the end of June at the earliest. We're grounded in Austin for a few more weeks.

Not such a bad deal, since I am dedicated to spending much of my time cooling off in the pool or on the boat. The doctor said to rest and I MUST follow doctor's orders, right?

Remember when I shared in February that certain liver enzymes originally tested at a dangerously high level of 1985? (Pretty scary!) It's nothing short of amazing that those numbers have been consistently coming down, down, down. A normal level is 130, and today I received the test results that my new level is 159.

Yes, I said 159 - a miracle in itself. Now I'm focused on staying the course until we return to MD Anderson on July 30-31. High hopes!

So as my birth-day comes to a close, I am falling asleep with a BIG smile on my face:

One more milestone achieved! On to the next event...

> Sleep well,
> Karen Strong

"Happiest of birthdays, my friend!
You always do what you say you're going to do,
so no surprise you're celebrating your 69th birthday!
I'll be saying the same thing next year!
Enjoy every moment and keep inspiring us all
with your positivity and continuing success!"

Pam W

T.G.I.F. – ANOTHER ONE
colorado fires devastating

IBM has woven itself into who we are, who we become...
I have nothing but fond memories, and meeting you along the way
definitely makes my highlights reel.
Keep your head and heart strong, and your body will follow."
Marlene H

June 15, 2018

Another busy and revealing week. Last week, I felt great after a full week of no chemo and no nupagen shots. I had energy, felt like my old self and actually began to have an appetite again. I thought, "Wow! this is pretty amazing."

Then Monday, I couldn't get chemo because of my low blood count. Back to nupagen shots Wednesday, Thursday, Friday, and back to nausea and total fatigue. But at least I know why... and now I'm ready for "3C."

Monday and all that the two-week cycle entails. Of course, the doctor has said no more nupagen-free weeks. So back to my "new normal" - which is pretty tolerable. I just have to keep the target in focus: the next visit to MD Anderson on July 30.

We couldn't go to Colorado this week because of the tragic fires in Durango and the high winds that brought terrible, smoky air to Camp Owen CO. The smoke is so bad that people have been suffering with eye, nose, throat, and lung issues. I can't travel there until the air clears when the fires are under control.

The fires have now burned 35,000 acres. How devastating to lose so much beauty, so much foliage and trees (which won't regrow in my lifetime). Fortunately, I don't think anyone has died, but the aftermath will be with us for years.

The good news: they are supposed to get a big rainstorm tonight and tomorrow which will, I hope, contain or possibly quench the fires. We're now rescheduled to fly to our haven on June 28. Fingers crossed.

Our new little grandson, Ford, is two weeks old today. What a cutie, such a blessing, and a true example of the circle of life. However, this has brought my grief over Blake to the surface, and I will admit to a resurgence of uncontrolled feeling of loss over my 'baby.' I think I could have doused those Durango fires with the tears I have shed just in the last week.

I don't know WHY this week, but I'm trying to go with the flow and work to get back into balance. I wish I knew an easy way to do that. I guess it is time to see my Shaman again. She should be back from Peru in another week.

Many of you have been interested to know "What is a Shaman, and why are you going to her when you are in traditional therapy and doing so many alternative activities?"

It is amazing to hear about an expanded belief system of the afterlife based on ancient healers and philosophies. As I've learned more about new beliefs and healing practices, I've also discovered this new perspective is very aligned with Christianity and provides a much expanded view of our bodies and minds as powerful self-healing entities; so enlightening, enriching and empowering.

I will go on long-term disability on June 19. And oh, what a onerous and time-consuming process to shift everything over. I will no longer get paid by IBM and my LTD pay is ½ of what I've received previously, but still, what an amazing benefit not offered by many companies today.

I will also no longer be covered by the IBM group Aetna policy we've held for years. I've spent about 20 hours over the last 10 days trying to reach people who know what I need to do. It is just a good thing I'm not so sick that I can't still use my IBM Exec skills to navigate the new systems.

Howard and I spent 2.5 hours today trying to figure out which new medical and dental policies we need to sign up for, since ALL my benefits will expire on June 30. We have to submit new tax forms, cancel HCSA and stock purchases, complete six applications for the new medical, dental, and RX plans, +++.

And the worst part is IBM won't be paying part of our new medical policies, so our monthly medical premiums will double. Gulp. And we'll see how much of my cancer bills will be paid under the new individual plans.

The most distressing part of all this is that after 18 years, I will no longer be an IBMer. I have to return my laptop, and lose access to all that goes with it. I won't have kowen@us.ibm.com any more - so to reach me, please shift my email to kowen@kaemark.com. I'm also going to need a new computer and transfer all my "stuff" in the next two weeks.

I feel like I'm being cut out of the village and losing part of my identity. A significant chapter in my life is closing, and my own, unique Employee ID # will no longer be mine. Quite unsettling and feels so 'final.' I didn't anticipate this visceral reaction, but IBM has been a profound differentiator in my and Howard's lives, so it is hard to close this very interesting book.

Another big change: I have now lost 50 pounds without dieting, a new and shocking phenomenon in my life. I must admit, dieting would have been my preferred choice, but life and death puts a new twist on the whole weight thing. My doctors don't want me to lose more weight, but I can't help it. When food tastes like metal or cardboard and when you really don't feel like eating, it's tough to shovel it in.

After age 50, I'm having to clean out my closet and get rid of my large, medium, and small sections of years worth of clothes. I have piles and piles of castaways. I've given stacks of clothes to benefit the Battered Women's shelter. I've given many better items to friends and will offer the top half of the medium-sized giveaways to even more friends this week. (Then I'll resell the rest.)

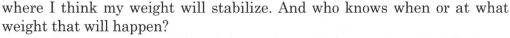

This is also quite an emotional experience and the closing of another chapter in my life. Since I will forever remain on my 'cancer diet' to fight the cancer, I'll never need my large or larger medium clothes again. This, too, is like parting with a very close, long-time buddy.

I'm keeping some of my 'couture' pieces to have altered when I get to the point where I think my weight will stabilize. And who knows when or at what weight that will happen?

I will miss the clothes I've collected from our worldwide trips. So many stories tied in with history: I just can't give up the gorgeous beaded gown I had made in Singapore, or, when AA lost my luggage in Geneva, the cocktail outfit I had to buy my first day at IBM. I had to shop for an outfit for the Executive Summit cocktail party that very first evening. Shoes, underwear, and an outfit in 1.5 hours working with a clerk who didn't speak English and I had no idea what their sizes meant.

The same happened in Santiago, Chile. So many memories tied to the coat from Estonia, or the custom clothes in Hong Kong, or the ski outfits from Beijing, or, most disconcerting to my sons: the Brazilian bikini in Rio (which I haven't worn north of the equator) - and on and on - what special stories woven into all these fabrics.

I've decided to keep my totally inappropriate Brazilian bikini - Don't come over unannounced when I'm floating in the pool, boys!

Well, I've become melancholy and am beyond tired, so good night, have a fabulous weekend - and Happy Father's Day to all!

Karen Strong

"Love and more love your way.
So much on your plate!!
One of your mantras could be *Karen Strong*,
and it would be so helpful. You are a woman of Power!!"
Alegria

Back On Track With 3C Treatment
a gift that keeps on giving

"You are amazing!
God has this, and your faith, determination,
and fight are going to get you through this.
Blake is your guardian angel.
Look up and let him know you know he is there for you!"
Belinda K

June 18, 2018

It must be Monday because I'm vegging in the big leather La-Z-Boy chair at the Infusion lab. Good news: According to plan and good blood counts, I'm here getting pumped full of my usual chemo cocktail. Bad news: I'm here getting pumped full of my usual chemo cocktail, which means the beginning of the three days of chemo infusing into my body. But Dr. Shimkus says I'm doing well, so we are 'all systems go' to leave for CO on June 28, subject to blood work next Monday.

I also get so much accomplished when I'm tethered to an infusion pump. It doesn't hurt; it just makes me sleepy and light-headed.

We had a calm, pretty uneventful Father's Day for Howard. He chose to stay home and watch AR beat UT in the college baseball playoffs and to watch the US Open. We did see or hear from all the kids, and I floated in the pool and napped and read, so it was pretty relaxing for me, too. We also got some much needed afternoon rain.

Yesterday was also the nine-month date of Blake's passing—and Howard's first Father's Day without him, another emotional hit. I pray Blake is truly free and happy in God's heaven, because we miss him more each passing day and my shattered heart is still in pieces.

NOT new news: I have no hair!

And since it is so hot, I often opt for total disclosure: no wig, no hats, no scarves. In fact, Howard has now decided that he thinks I look beautiful and exotic without hair. This from the man who would never ever let me cut my hair short.

My grandchildren are getting so used to their bald Nana, my shiny pate doesn't even phase them, not even my little 16-month-olds, Amelia and Brazos. Little Brazos loves to rub his tiny hand on my stubbly head while smiling so big. I've even thought of having my head adorned with a henna design and maybe starting a new trend. And next would be a tattoo (*really?*)!

Our tiny prince Ford is now 2½ weeks old. Yesterday, he studied me very contemplatively while I talked to him incessantly to imprint my voice in his little mind. Now I have to convince Lisa to let me babysit for him before we leave for Colorado!

I'm working through the transitions to being an ex-IBMer - making progress every day. But the actual event is TOMORROW. Still seems so surreal.

Onward and upward one day at a time,

Karen Strong

"I agree with Howard. Beautiful!
But I have to say, your wigs look JUST LIKE the hair
I've seen you in the last 30 years...
A head tattoo?! I gotta see this!
Sounds awesome and adventurous.
Love you, Mom! Xo"
Jenny B Q

A REALLY GOOD WEEK!
on our way to camp Owen CO

June 24, 2018

REALLY GOOD WEEK - even though this was a chemo week. Only side effects: fatigue, mouth blisters. I hope this is a 'new normal' because chemo weeks just aren't usually this easy. What a wonderful blessing! Lord, hear my prayer: more 'feel good' chemo weeks ahead!

So much to do to close up the Austin house and pack to leave for CO this Thursday - but Whoo Hoo! So eager to get up there. We arrive Thursday night and I have a 9:00 AM appointment at the Cancer Center in Montrose, CO, on Friday morning. We'll be scheduling my chemo treatments for the 4th of July week and throughout the month.

Have a great week,
Karen Strong

"Yes!! Blessings indeed.
Your mountain home will bring so much
wholeness and joy.
I'm already missing you!!
Colloidal silver helps get rid of sores.
It's amazing!! Love you!!"
Alegria

Riding a
Rocky Mountain High
keeping up with Steven and family

July 1, 2018

We landed 'on time' Thursday afternoon to a windy wall of heat, like standing behind the jet engine, at an historic high temperature of 97° in Montrose. It was only 98° when we left Austin.

Steven and our little mini-Steven, three-year-old Liam, greeted us. Nothing is better than the unfettered joy of a child who is so excited to see Nana and especially his Papa.

After our standard restocking stops in Montrose, we headed up the mountain to our special Camp Owen CO where it was only 87°! And of course, with no A/C in the house, we're delighted when it cools down to the 60s at night.

As we were flying in, a huge band of smoky air was visible at about 30,000 feet, caused by the Durango fires, and when we landed, the dense brownish haze hovered over the mountains at our house. Then much to our relief, the wind shifted and the air cleared by the time we drove up the driveway.

It is now Saturday night and we are exhausted from our last two fun-filled days with Steven, Shannon, Westyn (6), Liam (3), and Brazos (16 months). Big highlight today when we all rode the Razr and 4-wheelers up to the top of the mountains at Governor's Basin for a great picnic. It is so much fun repeating the wonderful CO experiences with the grandkids that we created with our own kids. I'm loving every minute in our beautiful heaven on earth with Steven's clan - and feeling good, too (after a challenging last week).

Friday morning we met the oncologist and team at the San Juan Cancer

Center. We were very impressed; everyone there had already read my file and seemed personally invested in treating me through July-September. Next 3C infusion is this Tuesday thru Thursday- so great expectations going forward in search of my CBD with THC oil.

Friday afternoon, I visited my first "pot shop" in search of my CBD with THC oil. The professionalism of the dispensary and the knowledge level of the clerk was a nice surprise. I was able to find the IoVia tincture in my current potency - a great relief since I couldn't fly with illegal-in-Texas medicinal marijuana.

I'm already feeling better being in our happy place in CO. We've had spectacular sunsets made even more beautiful with a full moon and galaxies of bright, twinkling stars. Westyn and Liam are in awe of this spectacular view, especially since we were all sitting around the firepit, roasting marshmallows for s'mores!

More to come next week,
Karen

"My heart is full for you and your family.
God is so great, and it is wonderful to read about your adventures
in your happy place. The heavens are beaming healing vibes down on you!
Hugs and prayers for healing, comfort, and pain-free treatments!"
Belinda K

Bummer: Tuesday
luxuriating in our "ether chairs"

"Hope u r watching a gorgeous Colorado sunset right now!
Colorado is a healing place.
People have been going there for nearly 200 years
to bathe in the springs and take in the clean air.
It will do that for you, too.
Play some John Philip Sousa marches tomorrow and power on!
We are with you, Karen Strong!"
Kathy

July 3, 2018

Howard and I woke bright and early to a beautiful Colorado mountain sunrise and packed my chemo bag to make the trek to Montrose for my treatment today. A very friendly and professional staff welcomed us.

First things first, as always, blood work and vitals. Immediate red flag: High, high blood pressure (which we attribute to my shooting pain head-aches). Since I started chemo, I haven't had to take BP meds because the chemo has signifi-cantly lowered my BP. But today, BP red flags and sirens.

Then Dr. Kilbourne (Big Boss) came in and said, "No chemo today. Your blood counts are much too low."

Doctor not concerned yet, but watching closely. I have to remember "one day at a time."

Dr. K also said I need to slow down, rest more, and stay away from crowds, kids, and anyone sick. Good thing Steven's family is all healthy because I couldn't stay away from my darling Westyn, Liam, and Brazos while they are here.

That also means I can't go to the 4th of July parade in the morning. That's a bummer. Instead, I'll be at the hospital getting my shot - poor me, right?

It's a good thing we're at Camp Owen CO, our happy place. It is so easy to meditate and pray when we're sitting in our La-Z-Boy chairs (known to many of you as our 'ether chairs.' Howard named these chairs because he says as soon as you sit down, ether rises from the cushions to put you to sleep.)

This is a good place for me to recommit to all I'm doing. I knew I'd have setbacks; just didn't realize how many and how often. But we still have our eyes on the prize: a positive progress report at MD Anderson at the end of July (or maybe later, now that I couldn't get chemo today).

I am very committed to helping 'new' cancer patients get through those first shocking and overwhelming six weeks. Today the wife of a newly-diagnosed cancer patient called us. What broke my heart is that he is not FIGHTING, won't try anything alternative, and is rebuffing his wife's support and suggestions. I am so sorry he won't allow her to fight WITH him. This makes it such a challenging and lonely journey.

But what I came away with is such gratitude for my soulmate Howard (my loving appendage), my family, friends, prayer warriors, and supporters. Right now, I'm picking myself up to get back in the saddle to LIVE.

I will earn my name: *Karen Strong*. And YOU are a key part of my success journey - -

Have a Happy 4th of July!
Karen Strong

"Wow, Karen! You are an incredible role model for how to tackle this journey
and all it includes. Maybe Blake is your secret weapon,
your spiritual companion who gives you courage.
Thank you for the open way you share what keeps you grounded and hopeful.
You inspire all journeys that are hard to travel."
Janie C

THE BLESSINGS OF
BEING IN COLORADO
happiness is being with Jeff's family and reconnecting with so many IBMers

"So glad you are in beauty of Colorado mountains
with your children and grandchildren.
Thank you for sharing your journey with us, as you are
an amazing inspiration, reminding us to appreciate every day."
Lynn T

July 11, 2018

Cam (my former IBM partner) shared my story and Caring Bridge site with many of my former ISAC grads, and I am excited that so many of them

have reached out to me with great comments of hope and concern. Made my day. Thank you all.

And thank you all for the wonderful, inspirational cards and positive messages of hope, concern, and love. You are my inspiration.

Yesterday I was able to get my delayed chemo, but it turned out to be a tough day. Had an unexpected, bad gastro reaction that took two pills and a shot to get under control.

The good news is that I survived and feel much better today. Tomorrow, more blood work, plus removing my pump and giving me a new long-lasting nupagen-type shot that should minimize my continuous low white cell blood count. We'll know next Monday.

Having a wonderful time with my five-week old grandson Ford, as well as my beautiful granddaughters, Laney (11) and Riley (9). Jeffrey (our oldest son) is taking me to the oncologist tomorrow, and I'm so excited to have some one-on-one time with him.

So glad to be at our beloved Camp Owen CO - the weather has been glorious. We even valued the first rain we've had up here for many months; watching the storms over the mountains is truly a religious experience.

Fingers crossed for good results tomorrow.

Good night,
Karen Strong

"Fingers crossed. And legs and arms and eyes, too.
So happy you are enjoying family time in CO.
Thanks for the updates.
You ARE a warrior and an inspiration.
Sending hugs, prayers, hope, and love. XO"
Bonnie D

"You are a warrior, Karen!
We are all behind you, praying for you and being positive.
So wonderful that you are spending time with your family.
And a little baby!
Nothing like children to keep you smiling!
xoxoxoxo"
Rosemary L

WHAT A BEAUTIFUL
TUESDAY MORNING
6 days w/o doctors

"WOW!! Everything sounds so good.
I am convinced prayer is a miracle no one, nor any medication,
can duplicate. Using prayer and modern science together,
with a positive attitude, creates an unbeatable team. We love you."
Jeani & Col. John

July 17, 2018

It doesn't get much better than a spectacular, cool, sunny morning in the beautiful San Juan/Cimarron mountains of CO. God must have spent a disproportionate amount of time working on Rocky Mountain views because, though we are only a spec among His creations, we marvel at our 180° view over majestic mountaintops jutting into fluffy white clouds floating across a clear blue CO sky! God has shared a bit of heaven on earth with us.

Yesterday, Ma and Pa Kettle (Howard and I) made our usual back-road trek into the Montrose San Juan Cancer Center for the usual interim blood work. Great news - the new Neulasta shot worked and my white blood cell count is normal, along with everything else except my platelets and potassium. They are low, but high enough, and I'm taking meds to build up.

THAT means I don't have to go back to the center until next Monday for my last CO chemo before I go back to Austin next Wednesday and then to MDA. This week will be the longest stretch of time (6 days) I've haven't had to go to the doctor since my diagnosis in January.

And most important: Dr. Prasthofer (CO oncologist and hematologist) did a 'new-to-me' CA 19.9 blood test designed to identify levels of tumor markers and chemo effectiveness on tumors between the three-month cycles of blood analysis and CT scans. Of course I don't understand half of what he said, but I gather that all pancreatic patients have an elevated CEA baseline above 19.9 and that the goal is a lower number. While I don't have my baseline, my current # is 9 - a VERY good number; we are VERY happy and eager to validate my improvement at MDA in 2 weeks.

Dr. P said many non-cancer patients have a CEA #9 level (not sure what that indicates for me). Just remember, I'm recalling a verbal discussion that was like interpreting Greek, so I hope my statements above are 'right on.'

Regardless, we're flying high in anticipation. And I just know Blake is walking this journey with me! Stay tuned…

We're off to take Laney and Riley to lunch and to visit the Dennis Weaver Memorial Park along a beautiful gurgling stream near Ridgway. This is a memorial where hundreds of people have built cairns. A cairn is a stack of rough stones built as a memorial to a person or 'dream'.

We have decided to let each grandchild build his or her own cairn surrounding their 'names' signs at the entrance to our home. We are, of course, focusing on Blake and Averie. Laney, our beloved granddaughter, suggested the garden of cairns right here at Camp Owen CO.

Thank you to those of you who have figured out my CO address and continue to send special gifts and cards. I cherish every single contact (texts, emails, books, legal seafood, +++) and especially the ongoing commitment to prayer. I KNOW prayer is one of my special differentiators, and I am so grateful. I am now offering support to newly-diagnosed cancer patients. THIS is one of my new life's focuses. So may I ask that you add my new cancer-ridden friends to your prayer lists. And if you know anyone who could use an 'experienced' cancer-friend, please just send them my way. I really want to help others in every way I can.

Off to build cairns,
Karen Strong

P.S. Today is the ten-month anniversary of Blake's death. My belief and prayer is that he has found happiness and peace, surrounded by love. He is still so loved and missed by many here on earth: We LOVE you and MISS you, Blake.

"What a wonderful idea to build your own cairn garden.
I can't wait to see pictures of all the creations. Love you."
Kathy G

LAST 3C DAY BEFORE MDA
Summer days with Laney, Riley, and Ford

"You really do have a flare for writing.
Always knew you were wonderfully smart and articulate
but I love the way you write, too What is it about
Colorado in particular that makes me feel closer to God?!...
Loving the numbers and good news. Love you."
Jenny B Q

July 23, 2018

Good news is that I am sitting in the San Juan Cancer Center getting my bi-weekly chemo fix. My potassium levels were low again, thus another bag of fluids coursing through my body.

I always take first place in having the most fluid bags (four) flushing through me at one time, for taking six hours at one sitting for my regimen, and then having the external pump delivering chemo through my port for the next two days. Y'all know I don't ever do anything half way!

But hope today will be the last day I will need take this very toxic fulfirinox. The doctors have told me most patients can't endure the cumulative side effects of this poison more than six months, and I have fallen into this category.

I can't wait to get to MDA and see positive scan and blood results, and then we'll decide what the next stage of my healing journey will entail. Howard is very assertive that if the CT results are good, he wants me to take two months off chemo to rebuild my body. I'm not through with chemo in the mid-to-long run, but a break would be so welcome.

We've been having such a wonderful time with Jeff and family. I KNOW my Nana time with Ford has been so peaceful and healing: the best therapy ever. I must brag that when I hold Ford close to my heart and rock and sing to him, he settles down and sleeps peacefully.

He and I also have such great conversations; he is telling me so much, though I can't interpret. I will deeply miss my 'Ford therapy' when I leave on Wednesday.

And of course, Howard and I have both enjoyed our cherished Laney and Riley. Howard has shown a new nurturing side of being Papa with the grandkids this summer that I have never seen in him before. Could it be because he is now retired and sleeping well with his new CPAP machine? Regardless, the grandkids will never forget the lessons/memories of the summer of 2018 with Papa O, and hope with Nana O, too.

Homeward bound to Austin this Wednesday to 105° heat, and that is *not* heat index. Who said there isn't global warming? It was a record 92° in Ridgway a few days ago....

Lots of love and good times to all,
Karen Strong

"What wonderful news!!
The difficult times will pass, but the Miracles
and the magnificent memories you are giving
your family and friends have no end!!
Thank you, Karen!!!
Your nobility of Spirit, and your generous heart
inspire us so much!!
Love and prayers don't stop!"
Alegria

So Many Unexpected Issues
last time for freeze mode

"What a week you've had,
and what energy to make it all happen!
You rock!
Such a sweet card from Westyn. Thanks for sharing.
How special all the Nana therapy is for sure!
Stay positive, present, and purposeful! xoxo
Pam W

July 29, 2018

A fast and furious week - Last Monday-Wednesday, I endured what I hope will be my last fulfirinox chemo days. Monday was quite intense as I had the two-hour IV bag of potassium in addition to the 'regulars.'

Tuesday was all about packing for Austin and spending our last quality day with Laney, Riley and Ford. Then Wednesday, I had my chemo pump removed and proceeded straight to the airport. (As we were leaving CO, Laney (11), handed me a lucky penny to take with me to MDA - so special!)

Howard jinxed it by saying we hadn't had many challenging trips from CO - so guess what? We got stuck in Houston for six hours and didn't fall into our Austin bed until 2:30 AM. For a healthy person, that would have been challenging and exhausting; for me, it was pure torture.

After chemo and the Neulasta shot to maintain my white blood cells, I go into 'freeze mode', which means, while everyone is hot and sweaty, I am freezing to death and totally exhausted. By the time we dragged into the house, I was shaking... I was bundled under all our winter covers while Howard was sweating profusely.

After a few short hours of sleep, I was up at the crack of dawn Thursday to see my cardiologist to get my wildly vacillating blood pressure under control. After a quick trip to the RX, I arrived at my much needed appointment with my Shaman. She is so invested in me and so determined to help me, I was there for four hours Thursday afternoon. What an intense session with great results.

I had emotionally and psychologically regressed with my positive, go-forward mindset in the last six weeks and desperately needed a tune-up. And as she said at the end of the session, she had to "take the car apart and rebuild it piece by piece." But it worked, and I feel back on track and ready to face MDA tomorrow. The big three takeaways:

1) Walk in a field of grace.

2) I am a very different person than I was six months ago. Close the book on Karen 1, and focus on a new, more enlightened, and purposeful Karen 2, the Karen who will achieve so much more for the duration of my life.

3) Focus every day on GRATITUDE.

And the emotion I have now is supreme gratitude for all the support I've gotten toward the long anticipated results at MDA tomorrow and Tuesday. Thank you ALL for the plethora of beautiful cards and wonderful messages I've received this week. So many of the cards are from people Howard grew up with in Bedford, IN, as well as so many of Fran's (Howard's sister) friends, many of whom I've never met. (Fran put out the clarion card call on Facebook. Thank you Fran.)

I've also received many cards from Liz's dad's congregation, none of whom I've ever met. And my prayer warriors and 'regulars' have been hard at work. How could I not feel overwhelmed and grateful for the love, support, and prayers... so we are all eager to good news in the next few days. Fingers crossed again!

Lauren (Blake's wife) and I visited the new Dell Children's Hospital Mental Health Unit on Friday morning. Such an amazing improvement on mental health services for the Austin pediatric community. I'll write more about this later, but I believe we have found a phenomenal solution for maximizing Blake's memorial fund. More details over the next few weeks as Lauren and I crystallize our thinking. But as you can imagine, this was yet another very emotional meeting. Blake is and will always be so omnipresent.

Saturday: What was I thinking?

I hosted book club at my house Saturday night, but it was just what the doctor would have ordered. We had such a great time. As Howard said, "They were laughing and giggling like they were back in high school". Thank you, Book Club Babes. Laughter is definitely the best medicine and you girls definitely provide 'food for the soul.'

Sunday: Steven and Shannon brought my cherished Westyn, Liam, and Brazos for lunch and swimming. Being Nana is my best therapy! I just have to share the hand-made card my Westyn (six years old) brought me today:

> Dear Nana,
> You are amazing. I have been thinking about you! You are such a great Nana. I have a great time with you. I always think about you when I'm sad and it makes me happy.
> From Westyn

Pretty special, huh? As is the card Liam (three years old) made for me...

Past my bedtime - will send my results to all as soon as we get them Tuesday afternoon.

Expecting the best,
Karen Strong

"You are truly STRONG!
Your posts are a real gift and always feel like a blessing from the universe.
They define GRACE and are beautiful reminders about
the power of GRATITUDE.
Your ability to give back more during your journey
is both amazing and inspirational.
You are surrounded by healing LOVE!"
Sara V S

It's Great Day in Houston, TX
looking to the future

"FANTASTIC NEWS!!
You are an inspiring warrior surrounded by
strength of the love of family and friends."
Lynn T

July 31, 2018

Shout the great news from the mountain top!

I received my CT and blood work results from MDA this morning. Since my last visit on May 15, my pancreatic tumor has shrunk 66% and my main liver tumors have shrunk 46%.

We were not able to see my pancreatic oncologist because his flight from India was delayed; however, we did chat with his PA and my positive results amazed her. She said Dr. Javle would call us tonight or tomorrow to review our go-forward plan based on the new results.

She also that I would have to be on some type of chemo treatment for the rest of my life (since there is no cure for what I have, every doctor has told me the same thing). But she also expected I would be taking chemo for years to come: sort of a back-handed affirmation of my longevity, right?

I just know God and my Blaker had to hear all your prayers and support for me. Now we need to maintain the strong bandwidth of so many strong prayer warriors. You have made the difference!

Also, Liz called me this morning and to tell me about a very vivid dream and message from Blake. No one has had any signs from him since February, and I must admit I've missed his flash messages to members of the family.

But last night, Liz dreamed of Blake and Averie (Liz and Scott's daughter in heaven). Blake and Averie were in a field of flowers and Blake walked up to her and said, "Do not let Mom give up. I know there are times she has and wants to give up, but she has to keep fighting. We (he pointed to Averie) are not giving up on her. She can do this. Tell her she is more beautiful now than she has ever been and that we love her."

He hugged Liz and then called for Averie. Averie ran and jumped into his arms and hugged him so tight. Blake looked at Liz and said, "We love you, too, and be strong." Then Liz awoke and felt Blake's presence so intensely that she called out to him…

I've been doubly blessed by knowing Blake and Averie are happy and well, and by learning my great results from MDA. I just can't wipe the big smile from my face.

Lots of love and joy,
Karen StrongER

"When I saw the title of your post, I smiled,
and reading your post, my heart is full of hope and joy!!
Such great news! You're a fighter and have taken this head on
(as you do everything - so no surprise!) :)
Love that Blake and Averie make their voices heard!
I'm sure it brings additional strength and conviction.
Keep up the great work!"
Pam W

THE SKIES ARE REALLY BLUE AGAIN!
two-week vacation

"So great to hear these wonderful news!!!
I can feel your smile and your
beautiful energy through your words!
More blue skies ahead!! xoxoxo"
Beatriz F

August 4, 2018

Howard and I didn't realize how much this six-month journey has affected our subconscious minds. And for those who know Howard well, you know he has always stressed the importance of properly feeding and controlling our subconscious minds. Just ask any of our kids.

What does that have to do with me?

Since our great news in Houston followed by yesterday's discussion we had with Dr. Shimkus, my Austin oncologist, Howard and I have both felt lighter and brighter. Howard noticed me singing in the car (which I haven't done in forever), the skies look bluer and brighter, I can laugh at a good joke - and though I can't believe I'm saying this, my next three-month treatment plan doesn't seem so onerous (fingers crossed).

Dr. Shimkus, always very stoic and professional, showed some emotion yesterday when he smiled as he said my results for the last three months are extraordinary. In fact, when we looked at the 75% shrinkage in my pancreatic tumor since February, he noted that we should look at the total volume reduction which he estimated at 95%.

WOW! That had not occurred to us. Same logic would apply to the liver tumors.

What are we doing for the next three months?

First and really exciting: I'm getting a two-week pass on a chemo treatment to allow my body to rebuild. That's like a two-week vacation in Hawaii.

Then I'll resume my bi-weekly chemo regimen, BUT we will be eliminating the most toxic ingredients of my 'cocktail' and reducing the potency of the infusions to minimize my most troublesome side effects, namely my neuropathy and painful mouth sores. I will still have Monday infusions and continue Tuesday/Wednesday chemo through the portable pump plugged into my port.

Yesterday, the doctor also administered my monthly shot to minimize my GI issues and two antibiotics to resolve other ongoing infections. Clearly, I'm not out of the woods yet, but the results speak volumes and I am completely determined to continue my focus and progress.

As you know, there is no 'cure' for pancreatic/liver cancer, but since I am doing so well, I asked the doctor if he thought I might eventually be 'cured'. He smiled and said, "For pancreatic cancer patients, if you are still alive in 5 years (very rare), you are considered 'cured.'"

Hmmm, food for thought.

I left the best for last: Dr. S said I can have an occasional glass of wine! THAT alone speaks volumes.

Rest assured, dear children of mine, I will stick to my restricted diet. I'm not taking any chances on backsliding. AND since I have given all my 'fat' clothes away and can't go around in my underwear, I have had to go shopping.

Imagine my angst in needing to go shopping (-; though I'm only buying 'the minimum' because I need to see where I am in October). But for today, it is really fun buying smalls and size 8 jeans. Who'd have thought? I never could have imagined...

This week I'm sewing again, altering many of my fall and winter vests, etc., to take back to CO. (We'll see how that goes. Anything really good I'll be taking for professional alterations.) We're returning to CO Friday and will meet Scott, Liz, Carson, and Amelia for two weeks together at Camp Owen CO. Can't wait to see my AR grandbabies. We'll be there until end of September, so if you are in the Telluride area, come see us, y'all.

Enough rambling - have a great weekend.

Full of love, gratitude and joy,
Karen StrongER

"Wonderful news!
Keep the positive flow and the singing...
do a little dance every day, too!"
Becky H

Just Rockin' Along
and meeting with a Medium

"I have several pieces that need altering,
can I drop them off !?
Never imagined you at a sewing machine before!
I love you and Howard!"
Cookie B

August 11, 2018

It is Saturday night and I'm just finishing up three weeks since my last chemo, and I have another full week to go until my next infusion. I can hardly convey how good I've felt this week. I remember what it was like *not* to feel the effects of chemo and loving every minute.

We got back to CO yesterday, where it has cooled off a little and the weather is awesome. We're heading up to the mountains on the RZR tomorrow. Scott and our three-year-old grandson Carson also arrived yesterday.

Liz broke her foot last Saturday and the orthopaedist said she couldn't come to CO and probably needs surgery next week. So Liz's mom took Amelia (18 months) back to Kansas City. We'll know Monday if Liz needs surgery, but hope she'll be able to come up later this week. Liz's parents are supposed to join us next week with Amelia. I hope the planets line up for all this to happen.

But the biggest news of the week is my two-hour meeting with a Medium last Monday. Karen (her name, too) was recommended by my Shaman. I hadn't been ready to engage in this activity until recently, but I decided the time was finally right. And it was!

I asked for this session to communicate with Blake, and every minute was an amazing experience. Not only did Blake communicate, but so did Averie and MY MOTHER. Through the medium, Blake, my mom, and Averie shared so much information that no one else could have known about except my family. Right away I knew this was 'real.'

Blake is better than good, happy, at peace, and being his authentic self.

Averie is totally attached to Blake, and my mother has fully embraced both of them in her loving arms. Blake and Mom each told me that now is not my

time to join them and that I have a purpose to achieve in my life: to work with mental health on Blake's behalf, to be the matriarch for my family, and to counsel other new cancer patients.

It helped me so much that Blake said I could not have changed what happened to him: his journey is his alone and though we can't understand, he is living his destiny. Having been so close to Blake during this session brought me such peace, balance and connection.

And it was such a bonus to communicate with my mother. Blake passed eleven months ago. No one could have convinced me that my journey would include many of the new approaches and paths I've taken. What a rocky road, but one I continue to traverse in search of my new destiny.

And my close relationship with my Blaker is a big part of defining the new Karen.

Trying to walk in my field of grace,
Karen Strong

"What a truly amazing experience.
I am so grateful it has given you some peace and understanding.
Now, enjoy this week with your family and feel GOOD.
Love you."
Kathy G

Back To Chemo Tomorrow...
and two weeks with carson

"We are so excited about your plans to use
the Children's Hospital to honor Blake.
Love you!!"
Jeani S & Col. John S

August 19, 2018

My 4-week chemo hiatus ends tomorrow. It sure has been a nice break, but I'm ready to move forward with another lofty goal for my next visit to MDA in October.

I've had a great week with my little Carson here in CO - very intense keeping a three-year-old busy all day when his dad is in the next room; amazing two-week bonding time, and great therapy for me!

Howard and Scott have been working intensely on the business plan and execution schedule for Scott's new homebuilding company. I am so excited for this new opportunity for Scott, and for Howard (I think). This means he comes out of his semi-retirement... but it is great to see Howard and Scott working together.

It has been two weeks since my communication with Blake, Averie, and my mother with the Medium. Amazed the calm and peace I took away from that contact has sustained me, as we experience God's majesty across these gorgeous mountains at Camp Owen CO.

I do feel so close to Blake here, and I know he is with me. We just need to get rid of the smoke from the California fires!

As you know, one of my life's goals is to memorialize Blake's life through my work with mental health as part of my Healing Journey. Blake passed away 11 months ago last Thursday, and I am already trying to decide how to memorialize one year on September 17.

I also don't know how long I will be progressing so well or what God has in store for my longevity, so I decided to look at options for leveraging Blake's memorial funds (Go Fund Me) NOW. After prayer and exploration, I called Lauren and we toured the new Dell's Children's Mental Health unit. This facility is such an immense step forward for children's mental health in Austin and I am eager to be involved.

We are in the process of setting up the 'Blake Owen Endowment' which will then continue to grow. Blake will be memorialized on the lighted "Butterfly Wall" at the hospital, and we will dedicate a bench in the Healing Garden to Blake.

So I hope to have everything in place by September 17. I KNOW this is what Blake wants. Stay tuned for more details -

Staying positive each day,
Karen Strong

"Your plans for honoring Blake are awesome.
I am sure Blake is loving it somewhere.
Good to hear about your time with family in Colorado.
The mountains are so gorgeous. Stay strong!"
Raghbir K

GOOD NEWS AND...
a little bad news today

"Karen Sparky Strong, YOU are the one.
Blake would be so proud of you. Love, Love you."
Judy W

August 20, 2018

A successful day of my new chemo cocktail. Now we're waiting to see if the new plan will reduce my most significant side effects.

The 'little bad news' today was that my potassium levels were dangerously low (with risk of heart damage) and my blood pressure is high, despite my new BP medicine. Let's see what happens over the next few days on this roller coaster... nowhere to go but forward!

Re: the Blake Owen Endowment for the Dell Children's Medical Center Foundation. Mental Health Unit, I am touched and thankful for so many of you who have asked how you can donate. Howard and I will be eternally grateful for your support.

Please know that any amount will make a difference. I am working with the Dell Foundation this week to create a direct link for donations that I will share with you as soon as it is live. In the interim, if you'd like to donate now, here is the info.

Make checks to: DELL CHILDREN'S MEDICAL CENTER FOUNDATION

Send to: BLAKE OWEN ENDOWMENT
Dell Children's Foundation
Attn: Susan Hewitt
4900 Mueller
Austin, TX 78723

With so much love and gratitude,
Karen and Howard

Happy 48th Anniversary To Us!

48 years of making history - what a story

August 29, 2018

Today is a glorious day: Howard and I are celebrating our 48th wedding anniversary. Happy Anniversary to my dedicated, loving soulmate.

As I absorb the beauty of the CO mountains from my desk, I'm smiling as my mind jumps from memory to memory - and those of you who have shared our tumultuous journey know that I need to be writing that book!

The Lord works in mysterious ways; Howard and I have become even closer and more in love during this last year of grief, pain, and rebirth. He had one day of retirement before my diagnosis, and then he jumped right on to the roller coaster of this cancer ride (now seven months). I could not have survived without him every minute of every day.

Happy Anniversary, my Love - and as I've said for years, ILYF (I'll Love You Forever)!

Now back to my treatment protocol...

On August 20, I had my first reformulated chemo treatment designed to reduce/eliminate cumulative and intense side effects. However, this Plan B hasn't achieved the objectives. So what now?

My Austin and CO oncologists have discussed shifting to a daily oral chemo pill (xeloda), which is intended to attack specific cancer cells while minimizing overall body damage. I think we'll be starting this Plan C in about two weeks (not sure yet).

Then I'm scheduled to go back to MDA in early November for blood work and CT scan to see if the newest treatment is working. In the interim, time for faith, trust, and continued prayer.

Shifting gears is somewhat risky and very scary... into the world of the unknown again. Stay tuned....

> Taking it day by day,
> Karen Strong

"Fingers and toes crossed.
I pray that this new treatment gives you
the very best of results.
I think of you and pray for your healing every day."
Deb W

CHANGE OF PLAN
another Labor Day weekend

"Hey, my dear friend...
I look forward to reading your journal with great interest.
I always enjoyed your emails after you and Howard
came back from a trip...
writing is one of your many talents!
I am thrilled with your progress and inspired by your courage,
raw honesty, and perseverance.
Inspired but not the least but surprised!"
Di (Diane H)

September 5, 2018

Hope you had a great Labor Day weekend. I remember only too well how wonderful those three-day weekends were. Now I hardly know whether it is a weekday or weekend.

As a result of the holiday, I jumped out of bed Tuesday morning and headed out for my reformulated chemo cocktail. Alas, my white blood cell count was too low and my side effects have not abated, so the doctor said 'no go.' We're now on to Plan C. Starting next Tuesday, I'll be taking oral chemo pills (six per day), on for two weeks, off for one week.

The doctor said it will be several weeks before I'll be able to ascertain this treatment's side effects. Again, fingers and toes crossed.

This chemo pill is supposed to attack specific cancer cells and minimize the invasion to the rest of the body, thus yielding fewer side effects. Though apprehensive, I'm really excited and hopeful.

I can't believe how fast this summer has raced by. Having the kids and grandkids has been so therapeutic, especially strengthening those Nana bonds.

We also visited our dear Austin friends, the Rashes, at their beautiful home in Crested Butte for Labor Day, and tomorrow three of my IBM buddies and their wives are coming from Atlanta, New Jersey, and Toronto.

I can hardly believe they will be here, and I couldn't be more excited. Then to wrap up our summer, the Collises will swing by on their way to Lake Tahoe.

The best part of this summer is that my hair is starting to grow back. STARTING is the operative word. It is now about ½ inch long and mostly salt with some pepper. Nobody recognizes me at first but once they have, the consensus is I look pretty exotic and 'cool' with this new DO.

After all, as Laney and Riley have said, "Many of the NY models wear their hair like this." There you have it, from the mouths of babes: I'm a pretty cool Nana.

The only one who doesn't like it is Howard... I'll post a new photo soon and let you be the judge.

> Loving the cool air and majestic mountains,
> Karen Strong

> "Everything is crossed and onto Plan C,
> Ms. Karen Strong!
> Enjoy the remaining days of summer -
> sounds like its been a great one.
> I've asked our colleagues to pass along my hugs to you.
> Let's see if they deliver - :).
> Enjoy the cool air and majestic mountains - sounds glorious, cool Nana."
> Pam W

Moving Forward with Plan C
trying new chemo pills

"You are a beautiful lady inside and out.
Prayers continue for complete healing and
that this new plan C is the miracle treatment.
God bless you and your family!"
Belinda K

September 11, 2018

Blood work good today. Starting chemo pills tomorrow morning. Will take up to two weeks to see if side effects are reduced as expected. Glad to be moving forward...

Many of you have seen the photos my IBM buddies posted on FB over the last five fun days and have commented on my new 'do.' So I've now posted 'the new Karen' on this Caring Bridge profile.

Yep, I sure do look different. In fact, when I picked up my friends at the Montrose airport, they didn't even recognize me.

Feeling so good,
Karen Strong

"So wonderful that you had a great time with the old IBM gang!
You look beautiful!"
Beatriz F

Moving Past Monday
a year like no other

"I'm happy to hear that your "first anniversary"
of such a difficult time is behind you!
Thanks for the updates. You are such an inspiration.
And... I love your new photo and new 'do!'
xo Sending hugs"
Bonnie D

September 19, 2018

I wasn't sure I'd make it through Monday, one year since we lost our Blake. Despite my best efforts, I relived in my mind the last days of Blake's life over and over, which totally paralyzed me; there just are no words...

What pulled me through were the many texts, calls, cards, and gifts y'all sent. I felt your support and love as I struggled to push through my grief and pain: thank you so very much for every thought, prayer, and action.

This one-year mark also hit Howard harder than he anticipated, so we really clung to each other and finally made it through the dark and starry night until dawn brought new hope and the closure of a dreaded 'first.' Now to refocus on living each day to its fullest, healing, and achieving my life's goals.

Our newest mission is to partner with Scott and Liz in Sapphire Homes, our new home-building company in Northwest Arkansas. Needless to say, this is keeping Howard quite busy - a good thing.

I've now been on the chemo pills for a week today, and all is well. I'm feeling tired and having some gastro issues, but compared to all the side effects of my past six months of chemo infusions, I'm a new person. The proof will be in the pudding over the next two months until I go back to MDA in November to ascertain if this new med is further shrinking my tumors.

I do know that Blake is supporting me each and every day of my quest. I've become a little lax on my diet, but I am committed to being 'better' as I don't want to undo all the progress I've made.

We're still at Camp Owen CO, but will return to Texas in about a week. I will miss God's glorious mountains and the peace and healing that being in this majestic beauty and isolation brings me.

We welcomed some long-time friends from Austin yesterday, and it's great to share this haven with them as Margaret is my spiritual 'advisor' and writes the most beautiful, publication-worthy prayers for me - again, a special gift.

Working to move forward,
Recovering Karen Strong

"We could come back to Camp Owen if it helps :-)"
John D

"Yes, living each day to its fullest.
You continue to be an inspiration to me. Hugs."
Kathy T

Feelin' Good and Going Back to Austin
doctors are my new family

"Karen Strong, that's such great news!!
Keep up the awesome work and safe travels back to Austin!
You are a wonder, woman!!"
Pam W

September 27, 2018

I had my last checkup with my CO oncologist yesterday and am happy to report all good news. For the first time in eight months of chemo infusions and the completion of my first two-week pill cycle, my blood counts and potassium levels are GOOD. In fact, everything is within the normal range.

And side effects? So much better:

1) I'm still tired and need naps (not such a bad thing),

2) I only had one mouth sore (vs. the usual four-five), and

3) a new one: sores on the soles of my feet.

I'm learning what to do to minimize the pain and prevent blisters, but this is sooo much better than I've felt since I was diagnosed. I'm still having BP issues, so off to the cardiologist in Austin Friday. Full speed ahead with the new regimen until we go back to MDA on November 5-6.

We're ready to go home to Austin later today. God is good and obviously has been listening to everyone's prayer requests. I also believe Blake is always by my side, lifting me up and encouraging me to work hard and be strong.

I've decided we should invest in a vitamin and supplement company. It almost takes a spreadsheet to take all the liquids and pills in the right dose at the right time. This is definitely hard work - but so far worth every gulp.

Some of these pills are huge.

We have loved, loved, loved our time in CO with family and friends - and by ourselves. It is so peaceful and therapeutic in the majesty of these beautiful mountains with cool, fragrant CO air. God has provided just what the doctor ordered!

Have a wonderful fall weekend,
Karen Strong

"You are such a warrior!
Keep on fighting!
Prayers for quick relief and healing."
Fran

AND THE BEAT GOES ON AND ON AND ON
back to AR from CO via Austin

Keep the faith, Karen.
At a wedding yesterday we were reminded:
faith, hope, and love are super foods for your soul.
Xox
Trudy McC

October 14, 2018

Yes, I'm alive and kicking! Nice to know you've missed me!

Since last entry, we've come home from CO, unpacked, washed clothes, repacked, and headed to Fayetteville, AR, so Howard could work with Scott, and I could see Scott and Liz, and help them with my all-boy Carson and adorable Amelia. A fast and furious trip. Now we're home for a week before we head to the east coast for a friend's daughter's wedding.

So what's happening during this 2nd chemo pill cycle? Ugh, more side effects. I have developed a hypersensitivity to UV light, which is all outdoor light, whether it is sunny or shady.

To quote the doctor, "The sun is your enemy."

I'm supposed to cover up head to foot when I go out and slather 70 sunscreen on any exposed areas. On my hands, arms and chest, I have dark red blotches - I'm not sure what leprosy looks like, but that's what I feel I look like; but at least I'm not contagious.

The other side effect is blisters on the soles of my feet and palms of my hands, and this morning I woke to the biggest blister I've ever had on my foot. This is the side effect I've been dreading as this may mean I can't take the pills for another cycle. I'll find out tomorrow when I talk to the oncologist again.

I saw my ophthalmologist Thursday and am glad to report my vision issues are caused by extreme dry eye: Did you know dry eye is an actual disease? Well, now I know, so will be on prescription drops.

Then I visited my cardiologist because I haven't been able to get my blood pressure under control, so I'm now going on a new med. Pray it works.

Other than these issues of the week, I feel pretty good. The sun sensitivity is pretty stressful to me as our entire lives in TX and CO are outdoor-centric. I'll just keep tackling each challenge as it arises.

Howard described the situation as whack-a-mole. Pretty appropriate and I'll just keep whacking each 'mole' as it arises. And the beat goes on.....

Appreciate you!
Karen Strong

"I SO agree. Whack-a-mole it is.
I am praying for you on all fronts.
That whole allergic-to-sun thing and the blisters on the feet
are not fair! But this whole thing is not fair!!
You are amazing... keep up the awesome work and attitude.
Hugs to you! xo"
Bonnie D

Haven't Forgotten to Write
next stop: MD Anderson

And now these three remain: faith, hope and love. But the greatest of these is love.
"May you be embraced in love, lifted up in prayer and
cherished in every moment. Much love and hugs!"
Marianne C

November 4, 2018

I haven't written because I was waiting until after our next visit to MD Anderson, which is tomorrow. However, I thought I should update y'all that the day after I wrote my last entry on October 14, the doctor took me off my chemo pills.

I was so upset that I had such terrible reactions with the ugly red blotches and then the awful blisters on the bottom of my feet. Those foot blisters marked the end of that chemo pill regimen.

I haven't been on anything for 3½ weeks, and other than my liver 'talking' to me a few times a day, I've been feeling great.

We are going back to the unknown tomorrow in Houston. We will get the results of tomorrow's CT scan on Tuesday and then decide what the next step in my future is. I must admit I really don't want to go back to bi-weekly infusions, but that is probably what will happen. So keep me in your prayers tonight.

I'll be sure to post my results Tuesday-

> With love and gratitude,
> Karen

"Sending you big hugs and sending up to God the big prayers for
His guidance with the doctors tomorrow. Prayers for you always!"
Belinda K

GREAT NEWS!
Whoo Hoo! Glory to God!

"Whoot Whoot!!!
Beyond thrilled at this news!!
Way to go, Team Karen Strong!"
Jane B

November 6, 2018

Glory to God for all your support and prayers!

Just received my positive and awesome results. Pancreatic tumor is barely perceptible, liver tumors have shrunk 44% more since July and peritoneal cavity is resolved. And cancer markers have gone from 74 to 12 since July 30 (They started at 1200 last Feb).

As a result of all these improvements, no chemo for the next two months. Then we'll come back and redo all the tests to see what's going on.

We are so amazed and excited. Thank You all for All your prayers, support, +++. We wouldn't be here without you!

With love and gratitude,
Karen Strong

"Truly a miracle."
Glen B

"Wow - incredible!
I'm smiling from ear to ear :-)"
Cameron S

Secret Revealed!
cross my heart: dog-dewormer is a key part of my regimen

"Amazing! You should have the sign
"whatever it takes to help the miracle along"
tattooed to your forehead.
Happy Birthday, Howard!"
Marion M

November 16, 2018

Today is Howard's 71st birthday - and an absolutely beautiful fall day. Since my great news at MD Anderson last week, colors are brighter, smiles are bigger, I am enjoying every little thing, and I have been loving life. I am planning to be here for Howard's every birthday for years to come!

Now I have to confess my best-kept, life-saving secret.

In addition to the broad scope of programs, regimens, and tools I embraced during the last ten months of my cancer, I did not reveal what could be key to my amazing progress. I don't believe the chemo treatments alone would have carried me to this point.

Last March, Lisa's (my daughter-in-law) mother and stepdad shared guarded information with me about their friend in Oklahoma City who had been dismissed from MDA after eight months of unsuccessful treatments for lung cancer that had metastisized. MDA doctors told Joe they could do nothing else for him and he had 30-60 days. When Joe returned to Oklahoma City, a vet encouraged Joe to take dog dewormer.

Yes, dog dewormer, which had shown to help cancer patients recover from cancer. To read Joe's amazing story, go to mycancerstory.rocks.

With nothing to lose after my terminal prognosis, I started taking Panacur C last April.

After all, dog dewormer is similar in formula to dewormers used with children and to the meds given to adults traveling to Third World countries. Panacur C kills parasites and cancer is a parasite!

Of course, I was afraid to tell my doctors about the dewormer, thinking it would disqualify me from any trials and new procedures. But after my great news last week, when my pancreatic oncologist told me no more chemo for two months, I said, "I think it's time to share a secret with you. I've been taking dog dewormer."

Without missing a beat, Dr. Javle said, "I've heard about that. There's nothing in the dewormer that can hurt you, so if you think it is helping, continue to take it."

And I closed with, "I will."

After considering my doctor's response, I decided he knew more about it than he could say. He must have already known the ingredients or would not have told me it wouldn't hurt me.

Aha, what a detective I am!

I'm still taking my Panacur C and will be happy to share all that I've experienced in my ten-month journey with any cancer patients willing to step out of 'the box' to get well. I'm here to help!

In addition to continuing with many of the regimens and practices that have brought me to this great status, I will sprinkle dog dewormer on my mashed potatoes this Thanksgiving - and give thanks for all my blessings, my family, and for all the love, prayers, and support that have humbled me over the last ten months.

As a result of my Dog Dewormer, my dear friend Judy Waxman has now added SPARKY to my name. My new name is K SPARKY Strong.

And that's the way it is and will be forever more!

> Have a wonderful Thanksgiving with your loved ones,
> A very grateful Karen SPARKY Strong

> "Whatever works!!!
> Glad you decided to try something that sounded
> more-than-a-little strange, K SPARKY Strong.
> Hearing of your great improvement
> is a wonderful gift for Thanksgiving."
> Nancy McC

Preparing For A Joyous Christmas
Ho, Ho, Ho!

"Your posts and positive updates
make me smile and encourage me
to embrace each day with a big hug and a happy heart.
Keep up the good work, Ms. K SPARKY Strong. :)"
Bonnie D

December 5, 2018

I want to share this year's very special Christmas card with YOU, who are near and dear to me and have supported me through this year's journey.

Let Heaven and Nature Sing!

Christmas will be forever bittersweet, laced with candy and coal. The Lord has severely challenged our family during the last two years, yet He has also blessed us.

On September 17, 2017, we lost our beloved son Blake at age 31 after he had been married only eight months. When we thought things couldn't get worse, I was diagnosed with Stage 4 terminal pancreatic and liver cancer last January.

What a difficult journey we've travelled!

Yet here I am: almost a one-year cancer survivor! I am so grateful for all the prayers, love, and support (hundreds of cards, gifts, texts, calls, +++) that have carried me through . . . and so grateful for my indomitable Howard, who smothered me with love and care when I was diagnosed the day after he 'retired.'

Howard is now starting a new business with Scott in AR. Whew! I can breathe again; even after 48 years of marriage, I espouse "For better or worse, but not for lunch." Neither of us really embraced that retirement gig – though I am on long-term disability while beating the Big C.

As we approach this Christmas, our Blaker, our angel Averie (lost five years ago) and my mother are celebrating God's goodness with us. The Lord has blessed us; I am a walking miracle, feeling great and even off chemo until January and hopefully beyond. (I'm still taking a plethora of pills and supplements and leveraging varied and unconventional treatments daily.)

Jeff and Lisa also welcomed our unexpected, beautiful new grandson, Ford, on June 1, for a total of 11 captivating grandchildren. Jeff/Lisa, Steven/ Shannon, Scott/Liz, Tiffany/Kyle, are rockin' it as parents and professionals.

I pray for their health and safety every night, and I believe my prayers are being heard. Surely, blue skies are in store for the Owen family in 2019. We have come together in a way only a devastated family can. I appreciate every day and love being an active, engaged Nana!

The day after Thanksgiving, I gathered our precious family at the Austin Dell Children's Hospital to dedicate the Blake Andrew Owen Memorial Endowment for the new cutting-edge Mental Health Unit at the Children's Hospital. This is only the beginning of what I hope will be a growing testament to how Blake wants us to make a difference in Mental Wellness.

Friends named me Karen Strong earlier this year, and I am proud to be that 'new' me (though still not sure about the gray hair). I am dedicated to continued recovery, to counseling new cancer patients (those first two months post-diagnosis are brutal), to supporting the new Mental Health Unit in Blake's honor, and to be the best 'Woman' (Howard's endearment)/ Mom/Nana I can be.

To do all that, I no longer sweat the small stuff!

May 2019 bring you love, good health, peace and joie de vivre!
Karen Stronger than ever and Howard

We wish you Joy and Blessings in 2019!

Merry Christmas from the Owen Family

(Impromptu Thanksgiving Photo)

Let Heaven and Nature Sing!

Christmas will be forever bittersweet, laced with candy and coal. The Lord has severely challenged our family during the last two years, yet He has also blessed us. On September 17, 2017, we lost our beloved son Blake at age 31 after he had been married only 8 months. When we thought things couldn't get worse, I was diagnosed with Stage 4 terminal pancreatic and liver cancer last January. What a difficult journey we've travelled! Yet here I am: almost a 1-year cancer survivor! I am so grateful for all the prayers, love and support (hundreds of cards, gifts, texts, calls, +++) that have carried me through . . . and so grateful for my indomitable Howard who lovingly smothered me with love and care when I was diagnosed the day after he 'retired'.

Blake's Wedding in early 2017 and his Memorial Wreath last Christmas

Howard is now starting a new business with Scott in AR - Whew! I can breathe again; even after 48 years of marriage, I espouse "For better or worse, but not for lunch." Neither of us really embraced that retirement gig – though I am on long-term disability while beating the Big C.

Howard and Karen with Jeffrey, Scott, Steven, & Tiffany at Blake's Memorial Bench in the Healing Garden. The plaque says, "May all who rest here find peace and healing. In honor of Blake Andrew Owen."

As we approach this Christmas, our Blaker, our angel Averie (lost 5 years ago) and my Mother are celebrating God's goodness with us. The Lord has blessed us; I am a walking miracle – feeling great and even off chemo until January *and hopefully beyond.* (I'm still taking a plethora of pills and supplements and leveraging varied and unconventional treatments daily.) Jeff and Lisa also welcomed our unexpected beautiful new grandson, Ford, on June 1 *for a total of 11 captivating grandchildren.* Jeff/Lisa, Steven/Shannon, Scott/Liz, Tiffany/Kyle, are rockin' it as parents and professionals. I pray for their health and safety every night, and I believe my prayers are being heard. Surely, blue skies are in store for the Owen family in 2019. We have come together in a way only a devastated family can. I appreciate every day and love being an active, engaged Nana!

The day after Thanksgiving, I gathered our precious family at the Austin Dell Children's Hospital to dedicate the **Blake Andrew Owen Memorial Endowment** for the new cutting-edge Mental Health Unit at the Children's Hospital. This is only the beginning of what I hope will be a growing testament to how Blake wants us to make a difference in Mental Wellness.

Friends named me *Karen Strong* earlier this year, and I am proud to be that 'new' me (though still not sure about the gray hair). I am dedicated to continued recovery, to counseling new cancer patients (those first 2 months post-diagnosis are brutal), to supporting the new Mental Health Unit in Blake's honor, and to be the best 'Woman' (Howard's endearment)/ Mom/Nana I can be. To do that, I no longer sweat the small stuff!

Owen Grandchildren at Dell Children's Hospital dedication of the Blake Andrew Owen Memorial Endowment benefiting the new Mental Health Unit.

May 2019 bring you love, good health, peace and joie de vivre!

Karen *Stronger than ever* and Howard

2019

COULDN'T BE MORE GRATEFUL FOR TODAY'S GREAT NEWS!
ringing in the New Year!

"This is such great news,
and I am so happy for you and your entire family,
who continue to fight
this damn disease with you."
Gigi R

January 14, 2019

Have you ever felt that time passes both slowly and at warp speed at the same time? That's how the last three months have seemed to me. Today arrived clear and crisp, and much to my relief, my oncologist reported all CT and blood results continue to be good, despite the fact that I have not had chemo for three months.

How awesome is that?

And yes, I am taking and will always take my dewormer.

Many of you have reached out and asked if I'm okay because I have not blogged in a few months. Honestly, I have continued to struggle with Blake not being with us for Thanksgiving or Christmas or his birthday last week. Once I compartmentalized his absence and my associated grief, I thoroughly enjoyed our family holidays, as you saw in my Christmas card.

After my solid results today, I am feeling better than ever. Dr. Shimkus wants to continue to track me monthly, since he saw a very tiny backsliding on a few of my numbers; but he assured me he will closely watch the trends going forward.

I have been helping multiple new cancer patients through the shock and confusion post-diagnosis, which is very fulfilling, yet emotionally challenging. Regardless, I am giving forward after my premier and successful cancer-fighting year.

I do realize that once a cancer patient, always a cancer patient. But I am supremely grateful to be in the <1% to survive the first year of pancreatic and liver cancer (first anniversary date: January 27).

Bless the Lord and all of you who have been so supportive in so many ways.

"Cancer" still takes up much of each and every day. I absolutely must keep stress at bay and continue with all my alternative regimens. Whew, it sure takes a lot of work, but obviously, my results are worth it.

I hope to hear from many of you in the coming months as you keep opening the surprising gifts of life. And if you know of any new cancer patients who could use some 'experienced' support, just reach out and touch me!

> With love, gratitude, and joy,
> Karen

> "Your grateful spirit is so inspiring to all.
> Thank you for being a fighter and a one-year survivor!
> We aim to follow in your footsteps."

> "So so happy! I'd do a cartwheel if I could."
> Susan R

A LITTLE BUMP IN THE ROAD
no, no, no, bump, bump, bump

"The bumps in the road and constantly being tested in so
many different ways. We're sending loads of positive thoughts,
laughter (just look at the coat of arms Carl sent),
prayers, hugs and love.
You have already earned Karen SPARKY Strong
a kizillion times over, as you're an amazing lady."
Lynn T

January 30, 2019

Just when you think the road ahead is smooth, oops - a bump. I'm still glowing in the aftermath of my last great CT scan results in early January. But, I received my January blood test results last Thursday and have been ruminating about the new bump in the road ahead.

My CEA test results (Tumor Markers) have been climbing slightly but steadily for the last three months. That is certainly not what I wanted to hear. So my Austin oncologist said we'll do more blood work in two weeks and if the #s continue to increase, we'll be considering retreatment.

But I say, "no, no, no," so I'll be extra vigilant in leveraging my entire arsenal of cancer-fighting tactics for the next two weeks.

What lots of cancer survivors have shared with me is becoming ever so crystal clear: Once you have cancer, it is a daily presence in your life. It is omnipresent forever, whether it is reattacking or lurking in dark.

Regardless, I continue to learn and try to comfort others who have called for info, comfort, and support. I must continue to 'earn' my name: Karen Strong.

Will let you know what's going on in about 2 weeks.

Love and gratitude,
Karen SPARKY Strong

"You are strong on the outside,
but have a sweet, mushy core.
Just like an M&M!!
Will keep praying for you."
Susan T

"Staying positive has carried you this far.
Smiling and laughing also gives you inner strength.
You are doing so fantastic!
Your support to others gives you strength as well.
Lots of hugs."
Patti H

Keepin' On Bumpin' Along
a beautiful blue-sky day

"Keep up the good work.
We are on our knees thankful for
the progress you have made and
will continue to make! Love you!"
Sandy P

February 15, 2019

Saw my oncologist this AM. Though my CEA # increased from 17 to 29 this month (normal is 0-4) and that is not what I wanted to hear. My doctor said all my other #s are so good and I feel so good that I shouldn't be concerned.

He told me to just keep doing what I'm doing and we'll reassess after my March CAT scan. So I'm loving and living life!

We're on our way home from a beautiful afternoon on the boat - and do I ever appreciate God's spectacular sunset we just witnessed.

With joy, love and gratitude,

Karen SPARKY Strong

PS. Still faithfully taking my dog dewormer!

"You are a testament of God's love and I always enjoy
reading your positive and uplifting messages.
Your inspiration and encouragement are contagious!
My thoughts and prayers are with you always.
Keep loving and living life!"
Belinda K

A TOUGH ONE TO WRITE
shaman diagnoses PTSD

"It's tough but let's face it,
you are pretty much a badass and
I know you will get all the support you need!
Miss you and love ya,
you continue to be in my prayers.
Keep kicking ass!!"
Rachel

March 7, 2019

I've been thinking about writing this journal entry for more than a week. I just couldn't decide if I wanted to share these thoughts.

But then I thought that if you are reading this, you are continuing to love and support me. And I reminded myself that I've made one of my life's goals to focus on furthering mental wellness in honor of Blake.

A few days ago, my shaman sent me a poignant article on the impact of trauma and stress on disease. According to many sources in mainstream medical literature today, anywhere from 60-90% of illnesses have stress-related emotional underpinnings that can be translated into one word: trauma.

Current thought is that we can't permanently cure disease without addressing trauma. Psycho-spiritual trauma needs to be addressed and treated. For those of you who have been close to me over the last six years (and even before), you know that Howard and I (plus our family) have experienced extreme trauma. It really isn't too surprising that the Big C attacked me 13 months ago.

What does this have to do with Karen SPARKY Strong today?

Last week, my therapist diagnosed me with PTSD. From losing Averie 5½ years ago, to arson at Kaemark (our manufacturing business) that took Howard 2½ years to rebuild, to the worst of all: losing our beloved Blake in September 2017, and then being diagnosed with terminal cancer in late January of 2018, Howard, our children and grandchildren, and I have been violently whiplashed.

Praise the Lord I am physically doing very well – but –unrelenting grief, depression, fear, and anxiety have reared their ugly heads. And guess what? I am having to work just as hard at getting psychologically balanced and healthy as I have had to do for the last 13 months to become physically healthier.

I'm realizing my PTSD is as serious an illness as cancer – and I need to focus all my efforts and skills on continued recovery and mental wellness. My therapist is awesome; she is looking for a PTSD specialist for me. And I do believe Blake is with me always and wants me to be happy and peaceful, and that we will be together again in due time.

It is so important to understand better the importance of aligned mind and body wellness. You can't have one without the other. I will have my next CAT scan next week, and I am fearful.

Will my resurgent grief and anxiety affect my cancer results? I hope not, but that's why I need to conquer this PTSD asap.

It will be with God's will that my tumors continue to shrink, but that will happen only if I am positive, faithful, and mindful. So back to my more disciplined life of diet, meditation, therapy, mindfulness, prayer, exercise, devotionals, stress avoidance, and laughter!

Such an overwhelming task, but I guess I'll have to JUST DO IT!

> With love and gratitude,
> Karen Sparky (*remember my dog dewormer?*) Strong

> "Much prayer offered for you last night after reading your update.
> Read Psalm 139 this morning and what a wonderful reminder
> of God's omniscience and omnipresence,
> how God sees and knows the details of our lives
> as our Creator and even the thoughts of our hearts
> before we are ever able to verbalize them.
> Nothing escapes His notice.
> Praying both for your physical needs and that
> your inward needs find strength, encouragement, hope,
> and rest in Christ who is able."
> Terry T

A New Path Along
The Journey
staying focused on
my mental recovery

"I love the fascinator and the photo!
Just lovely!!
You make a difference to all who know you.
Positive prayers for continued healing on ALL fronts!
Be well, my friend."
Jane B

March 12, 2019

I guess I hit a hot button with my comments about my PTSD. I am so touched by your knowledgeable outreach, awareness of the mental/physical alignment of trauma and disease - and an understanding of the importance of new approaches to mental wellness and treatment.

Though my situation is very different than Blake's, sharing my mental recovery is just gettin' on down another path along the road. And 'sharing' is also such an important element of my mission. So stay tuned...

On another topic: I have hair (though it is still short): lots of very thick, very curly, very coarse, and very uncontrollable BLOND hair. But I love it because it is mine!

l-r: Genie (sister), Shannon, Riley, Karen,
Westyn, Laney, Amelia, Liz, Lisa

This photo is from a Valentine Tea. Notice the very chic Fascinator? (How could you not?) Not surprising that Howard was mortified that I would wear this funny-looking hat anywhere.

BUT guess what? Karen Sparky Strong is immune to what any one else thinks. So now the goal is just willing my hair to grow longer faster.

My quarterly CT scan is tomorrow afternoon - with blood work and re-sults at my appointment with Dr. Shimkus Thursday afternoon. I expect nothing but good news and another three months of avoiding further chemo!

I find it so amazing that another three months have sped by and I am still feeling so physically healthy. It is also very fulfilling that I have been 'sharing' with lots of new cancer patients in my efforts to help them navigate those first few shocking and cloudy months of post-diagnosis desperation. I so want to make a difference.

I'll be back in touch Thursday nite.

With love and gratitude,
Karen Sparky Strong

"You look adorable, Blondie!"
Pansy F

"Karen Strong, you will rock whatever you wear
and know Howard will love it!
Opening your feelings, your heart, and your soul,
and sharing your story, your joy, and your sadness,
along with your PTSD, is very courageous.
As you heal your body and soul,
you are helping all of us in more ways than you realize.
Sending positive thoughts, hugs, and loads of love."
Lynn T

"Well, you know blondes have more fun!"
Nancy McC

IT'S A WONDERFUL LIFE
stable sounds so good!

"I love your new hair! You look like a princess in that photo.
I learned to wear fascinators and hats
"whilst" (British word) living in England... they are fun.
I'm glad to hear that you are doing well, feeling stronger,
and growing your own hair! You are an inspiration to
all who know and love you. Keep up the great work, Karen Sparky Strong!"
Bonnie D

March 14, 2019

Hallelujah! I feel so blessed. .

Just got my CT scan results: no change since December. The word STABLE never sounded so good.

Blake and my mom are whispering in God's ears, and He is also 'hearing' a barrage of prayers for Karen Sparky Strong that He can't ignore.

So many blessings, including freedom from chemo for at least three more months, and I get to keep growing my own hair.

It's a beautiful day in Austin. How better to celebrate than to head out to the lake and give thanks for the beauty of this earth - and my continued life here with all that means so much to me? Days don't get much better...

Sailing away with love and gratitude,
K.S.S.

PS. Now back to my focus on mental wellness

"Such great news!!!!! Yay!!!!
Enjoy the day, the weekend, the year, the life!"
Beatriz F

Things Not Going Too Well
infection not welcome

"So happy you are continuing your baby steps forward in your recovery.
Bentonville is a wonderful area to live.
When Sara made her *Lizzie Documentary*, we went to the
Bentonville Film Festival. Everyone there is so warm and friendly.
Happy for Howard and his new career!
Best wishes to you and lots of love"
Patti H

April 28, 2019

Happy Spring!

I caught my first real infection since October, but after steroid and antibiotic shots and oral antibiotics, I'm almost to the goal line of feeling better again. That said, I am so blessed that I had been doing so well- except for being tired all the time.

Next blood work: two weeks. Keep the prayers coming.

So much is going on. As you know, Howard is starting Sapphire Homes of AR with Scott and Liz. And if you know Howard, we never do things in a small way! We bought a small subdivision and are now building our model and firsts specs in Bentonville, AR. We'll launch our new web site in about a month with everything you would ever want to know: SapphireHomesAR. com

We also decided we need to be in AR most of the time for the next few years to build this new business, so to provide stability and a 'home' away from home, we have bought a lake house in Eureka Springs and are selling our beloved Camp Owen CO (very sad and emotional). It's pretty obvious that the extreme CO cold and altitude are no longer my friends, so we are excited to begin this new adventure at Camp Owen Ozarks.

And the best news is that I am here for the journey!

Several months ago, I 'fessed-up that I have been taking dog dewormer (PanacurC) for over a year now. The web site to find out all about this is: mycancerstory.rocks authored by Joe Tippens.

The secret is out: Joe was featured on KOCO News 5 at koco.com (ABC affiliate) on April 26. The video and articles are both online. Amazing Story. Joe has asked me to write my story for his web site; I've been procrastinating, but now that he needs more documented success stories, I'm all in.

I'll post a copy of 'My Story' here after I write it and send it to Joe.

Another hot topic: Blake passed away September 17, 2017. Y'all know the painful story of his mental demise for a year prior to his suicide. He had been taking the prescription drug Suboxone (for too long) which totally altered his brain. Despite so many doctors, psychiatrists, therapists, meds, diets, supplements, +++, Blake finally decided he would never be able to function again.

As part of my focus on mental wellness, I have communicated Blake's story and the irreversible mental and psychological agony Blake experienced even after he had physically withdrawn from prescription Suboxone. Then last week, our son Steven forwarded an article to us documenting a US Justice Department. Lawsuit Against Suboxone:

https://www.reuters.com/article/us-indivior-lawsuit/u-s-joins-lawsuits-against-indivior-reckitt-over-drug-suboxone-idUSKBN1KT2NW.

The next step in my healing process is to support this lawsuit! If any of you have any experience in this arena, please help me contact me. Blake's legacy is also an important part of my PTSD recovery.

I have been counseling soooo many cancer patients. Though these engagements with members of this elite 'club' (which no one want to join) are very emotionally challenging, my interactions are very rewarding. I believe I am making a difference in peoples' lives, and I truly believe this is one of God's goals for me. If you know anyone who is facing cancer, please feel free to give him/her my phone number and email address. I respond to every outreach.

Enjoying a beautiful spring day in Austin. Praise the glory of God!

With love and gratitude,
Karen 'Sparky' Strong

"So sorry about the infection but glad you are recovering.
You are such an amazing inspiration with all you do! Hugs."
Kathy G

More Not So Good News
CEA and CA19-9 numbers rising dangerously

"Beautiful letter.
Will be thinking of you on Monday and Tuesday.
You can handle whatever it is, Karen Strong!"
Susan W

May 9, 2019

I was all excited to share the news that my CBC panel was all good - everything within normal range. Then I just received my tumor marker test results (CEA and CA19-9) and I was shocked to see serious numbers going in the wrong direction. I immediately called my oncologist and he said, "Yes, I saw your numbers and I am very concerned. We need to get you in for a CT scan tomorrow or Monday and then come in within 24 hours of the scan. And you should start thinking about what type of treatment you will go back on..." and he rattled off four options.

Well, I don't want to borrow trouble, but right now I have no idea if/what treatment I will choose - need to know the pros and cons.

Please keep me in your prayers and thoughts for the next few days; needless to say, I'm scared and concerned. Just the thought of all those side effects again is giving me the heebie-jeebies.

Maybe the CT scan will not show growths as indicated by the tumor markers... After all, to date, I am in the <1% survival group - and I intend to stay there.

Changing the subject:

About a month ago, I received a call from the Dell Children's Foundation. Susan, the director, asked me to write an article detailing why I chose the Children's Hospital for Blake's Endowment Fund.

This is what I wrote:

I never dreamed that mental illness would touch my beautiful family of five healthy children. I had always prayed God would help me and their dad to raise them to adulthood in one piece with all limbs attached. Never did it even occur to me that our youngest, closest, and most amazing son Blake would become addicted to a prescription medication that would rewire and destroy his brain.

For a year, we watched him descend into a mental hell where he was depressed and anxious, suffered from headaches, cloudiness, and nausea, couldn't think or process, couldn't sleep or navigate the professional successes he had earned in the previous five years. (Blake had been North America Salesman of the Year in his division at IBM.)

And this was our son who had prevented two of his friends from committing suicide and was always helping others.

Blake successfully withdrew from the physical prescription drug dependencies, but he never recovered mentally. We searched for knowledgeable doctors, experienced therapists, vitamins, diets, in-patient and out-patient programs, and a hit-or-miss series of prescription drugs, never knowing for weeks on end which ones (if any) would help Blake or relieve his intense suffering. And we had to document his history with each new medical professional. It was a stressful and heartbreaking year.

And then the unimaginable: Blake took his own life.

The pain, agony, and grief our entire family has endured in the past year-and-a-half is indescribable. After a year, I felt we had to honor Blake's legacy and focus on helping others in mental desperation (regardless of the cause). Despite our research and work with Blake, we had not found a one-stop-shop for treating emergency mental health issues.

By chance I saw an article about the Dell Children's Mental Health Unit and quickly toured the new facility. And the rest is history. This leading-edge Mental Health Unit is one of the few 'one-stop-shops' in the country where desperate and mentally ill children/teens can be treated by an integrated team of professionals in one family-friendly facility.

With multiple funds given in Blake's name, we dedicated the 'Blake Andrew Owen Endowment.' We held a wonderful dedication ceremony where our other children, grandchildren, and friends could see Blake's name on the Butterfly Wall; we sat on Blake's bench in the Healing Garden, an outdoor paradise for healing mentally troubled souls of children at risk.

It was an afternoon that our family will never forget.

And we will always be grateful that Blake has been memorialized in perpetuity through the growing funds that will make a difference for children who will live and love as a result of the help received at this unique haven. Though it is too late for Blake, I KNOW he is happy we are helping others work toward mental wellness right here in Central Texas.

The plaque on Blake's bench says it all: "May all who rest here find peace and healing." - in honor of Blake Andrew Owen. And this is just the beginning...

Karen Owen

"You told your story of strength and survival!
Your perseverance to live and help others touched my heart!
A wise Godly man I know of died unexpectedly way too soon.
His family found this note on his desk.
I copied it as a reminder.

'Those who believe in a sovereign God
should be the least angry, the least anxious,
and the least fearful.
Fear Not.
God is the author and finisher of our stories.
He invites us to a calm trust.'

You are in my prayers!"
Mary C

PATIENCE IS NOT ALWAYS A VIRTUE
hear me roar

"YAS!!! I'm reading to Shawn right now.
He says good work, mama Owen!"
Jenny Q

"I feel sorry for any mole you and Howard decide to whack!"
Kathy R

May 11, 2019

I was seriously upset by Wednesday's tumor marker test results. As I shared on Thursday, my oncologist wanted me to get a CT scan ASAP. However, I couldn't get an appointment until next Monday and results until next Wednesday: not good enough for me!

So I managed to secure a scan yesterday morning, have results sent to my oncologist in two hours, and finagled an appointment with my doctor yesterday afternoon. (My position: *Just Do It*). I just couldn't bear the thought of waiting 5-7 days to know what is in my future.

Dr. Shimkus gave me some pretty good news yesterday afternoon - relative to what could be. ONE of my liver tumors has grown enough to produce the high-growth tumor marker numbers. It is very unusual for only one tumor to grow while the remaining tumors are holding steady, but then, everything about my cancer is abnormal. Dr. S wants to know why.

So we're going on the attack: cyber knife and radiation. First, the specialist will surgically biopsy the tumor and implant a 'bead.' Then the radiologist will target radiation on the deviant tumor and hope to blast it away with as little damage to the liver as possible.

Howard likened this course of treatment to Whack-a-Mole - and the doctor agreed. The hope is that none of the other tumors decides to misbehave for at least six months.

Dr. S wants to start immediately, so we're now subject to doctor availability. This course of action appeals to me a lot more than chemo - and I won't lose my hair again. I'm ready to move forward with faith and hope.

I'm still taking my dog dewormer and getting calls almost daily to help other cancer patients. For 'the dewormer story', the web site is:

mycancerstory.rocks

I have been truly touched by so many of your comments about my story of Blake. We are deeply grateful.

For those who have asked how to donate to Blake's Endowment, go here:

www.supportseton.org/dell-childrens/give

Then click on Blake's name in the drop down menu.
Stay tuned!

> With love and gratitude,
> Karen Sparky Strong

"I'm so sorry you re being forced to play
such a high stakes game of Whack-a-Mole.
And I am humbled by your fortitude, faith, and determination.
Keep on pushing against the system to ensure
you get the best cutting-edge treatment possible without delay.
Thinking about you and praying for you."
Judy H

"You go, girl! Way to take charge of the situation.
You must feel better with a plan in place now.
You're an inspiration to many.
Love and prayers your way!"
Deb W

ANCHORED IN AUSTIN
cyber knife radiation delays trip to CO

"Not sure how something so insidious can be hiding
within a person who is outwardly beautiful, vivacious, caring,
sweet, thoughtful. You are a miracle,
You will be called upon to continue your super powers,
which will be most difficult. Sending encouragement and love."
Nancy McC

May 18, 2019

Change of plans.

Not leaving for CO until the middle of June - at the earliest. Instead, I'm facing the knife: the cyber knife.

Next Wednesday, I'll have the liver tumor biopsy and have a tiny seed implanted in that deviant tumor. I will then recover for a week until another MRI and CT scan to ensure all is positioned well for 'the knife.' Four days later I will begin the series of five cyber knife treatments over two weeks.

At that point, I'll have blood work redone and hope my tumor markers will show healing. But the true results will be revealed by the CT scan in early August. Those results will determine whether or not I need to go on a broad spectrum treatment - like chemo or immunotherapy, etc. etc.

This unsettling resurgence of active tumor growth has really messed with my head. I must admit I'm struggling to get back into the mind space to WIN this new war. It takes serious focus, commitment, attitude, and prayer to stay in 'the Zone,' and I'm gearing up for the long haul.

Changing gears again:

Yesterday was the 20-month anniversary of Blake's death. Was it only coincidence that I received the published article from the Dell Children's Foundation? Probably not!

... I would like you all to help spread the word that there is help available... The Owens never imagined their beautiful son, Blake, would die of suicide. Blake was a healthy, successful young man who found himself at the mercy of prescription pain pills. He fought hard to kick his dependency—and he succeeded—but the pills had caused lingering mental health challenges.

Though Blake sought the help of doctor after doctor, none was able to relieve his intense suffering.

Blake and his family are not alone in their heartbreaking struggle. According to the National Alliance on Mental Illness, one in five children ages 13-19 have, or will have, a serious mental illness.

Thanks to your support, we've made it our duty to ensure no child deals with the pain and suffering of mental illness alone.

In one year of being open, more than 10,000 young people and their families have utilized the Grace Grego Maxwell Mental Health Unit at Dell Children's. Our services range from crisis management to medication management, and we're equipped to handle any case, big or small.

Please read Blake's mother's story about honoring her son through the Blake Andrew Owen Endowment for Mental Health at Dell Children's.

We hope you will take a moment during Mental Health Month to learn more about the life-changing mental health services we offer at Dell Children's.

Sincerely,

Susan Hewlitt
Executive Director
Dell Children's Foundation

*If you or anyone you know is struggling with thoughts of suicide, there's help. Please contact the Mobile Crisis Outreach Team at 512-472-4357 or call 911 and ask for a Mental Health Officer.

"Praying for strength and a strong will.
You have been an inspiration to so many who are fighting cancer along with you.
It is always an uphill battle, but your faith and strength
will carry you through. Look at all the things you have overcome.
You've got this.
Stay strong and positive, and trust your faith."
Mari L

MEMORIAL DAY – NOT
working with the
interventional radiologist

"If it takes focus, commitment, attitude, and prayer, you've got it covered!"
Kathy R

May 25, 2019

What a non-memorable week. I sure am glad it is now Saturday.

It started with the husband of one of my dearest friends, Lynn (and the father of one of Blake's closest friends, Joey, and Tiffany's childhood friend, Melina) passing away last Sunday. Death and funerals evoke emotions we'd all rather not address. My heart hurts for them, and I couldn't go to the funeral today.

Tuesday, I had my appointment with the Interventional Radiologist (creme-de-la-creme of doctors) to prep for my surgery next Wednesday. I thought we were discussing one biopsy and one gold bead to be inserted into my growing liver tumor in preparation for my upcoming cyber knife treatments. However, Dr. Bell did not like all the dark spots he saw on the ultrasound and scans (performed in his office). We had a very sobering discussion about the extended work he would perform during my surgery.

I woke up after a three-hour surgery Wednesday afternoon and learned that Dr. Bell had inserted seven gold beads and performed three biopsies of different parts of my liver - "a lot of trauma to your liver," he said. Howard drove me home in the typical post-surgical fog, and I fell into bed in a coma-like sleep for two hours.

And this is where the challenges began. My layman's version:

As soon as I plopped myself down in front of the TV around 7 PM, I doubled over in excruciating pain and could not breathe, a horrifying feeling. Howard called my oncologist, who ordered him to call 911 and get me in an ambulance to the closest hospital. (My wonderful neighbor, Dr. Ariel, also came over and said the same.)

The worst was that the EMS techs could not give me any pain meds because my heart rate and BP both dropped. Instead they started a fluid IV and my stats were rising by the time I got to the hospital. Another MRI and CT scan. First concern: fear of aneurysm in my lung.

But a different situation had developed: my liver was so traumatized, I had developed a hematoma in my liver, and blood was leaking into my diaphragm. Results: pain and difficulty breathing - but soon great drugs!

They wouldn't let me go home until the bleeding stopped and the hematoma stabilized. But I was in such la-la land, I didn't care until they moved me to a windowless room in the basement that felt like a prison cell. THEN I told them I wasn't staying. And I walked out of that hospital yesterday afternoon after they confirmed no more bleeding.

But I have been put on 'restricted activity' until I go back Wednesday for yet another MRI and CT scan to determine the exact cyber knife treatments.

And I'm still in enough pain that I'm actually obeying orders... but I'm down to Tylenol vs. Oxycodone.

I must admit I'm struggling with this regression: so much hard work. Dr. Bell also said I need to go back on my strict Cancer Diet, but not so strict that I end up with diverticulitis again.

I'm also meditating again, doing my affirmations, listening to my Cancer CD, focusing on my spiritual life, praying, taking supplements, seeing my therapist and shaman, continuing with PanacurC, and working to get my head back into believing I can Conquer this Cancer AGAIN.

I am trying to live with gratitude in the moment each day and yet I still need FAITH that good can happen and HOPE. I'm reaching out to you, my prayer warriors, to ratchet up the prayer intensity. And for you to tell me what else I can do.

What other treatments have you heard of? The doctors think I may have to go back on chemo after the cyber knife, but I hope not. I'm researching immunotherapy as one alternative, and I'll get my research analyst, son Steven, to get back in the research game after we have the results from cyber knife.

I guess I also need to learn patience. GGRRR!. And the hardest challenge of all: acceptance that I am not in control... Lord, help me!

Poor Howard - no boating this weekend, but he has nestled into his 'ether' chair (La-Z-Boy chair that puts you right to sleep) with another WWII book (his favorite). Tomorrow is our youngest grandson Ford's first birthday celebration - so we will be heading to Jeff's ranch.

> With love and gratitude,
> Karen Sparky Strong

"You're in my prayers. Stay strong.
We are only a phone call away!"
Susan W

GRIT AND GRATITUDE
rapid remodel of
Owen Lake cottage in AR

"I read your posts and get courage, from you.
I receive strength, from you.
Your quest empowers many others as well.
You are not in this alone.
'Always remember you are braver than you think,
stronger than you seem, and loved more than you know'.
p.s. and stay away from U-Hauls!"
Rosemary L

June 7, 2019

First and foremost, thank each and every one of you for your comments, love, support, and prayers. You keep me motivated, and I KNOW your prayers are working to carry me through whatever God has in store for me.

A week after my unpleasant surgery (ten days ago), I had another CT scan and MRI. I still had swelling and that nasty hematoma in my liver. To my disappointment, the doctor said I could not start my cyber knife treatments for at least two weeks.

Not being a patient individual nor wanting to sit around just waiting for medical treatments, I decided to skip town. We packed up a U-Haul trailer with the first of many loads of 'stuff' for our new-old lake house. We headed NE about five hours after my disappointing doctor appointment and were cruising along quite nicely when we blew a tire on the U-Haul trailer.

Now THAT is NOT a good experience: a dark highway in the middle of an Oklahoma Indian Reservation at midnight with 18-wheelers whizzing by at breakneck speeds. After much ado, we found the U-Haul emergency number (they really don't want you to find it).

At 1:30 AM, the posse came to change our rim and tire, and we were on our way for a few minutes until a sheriff stopped us for a burned out light on the trailer... grrrr. But he sent us off with only a pleasant warning.

We arrived sleepy at Scott and Liz's at 4:30 AM. I will admit I didn't feel well for the next few days but stayed focused on minimal physical activity, diet, meditation, prayer, and...

I am working to complete the world's fastest remodel. Since Monday, we have had as many as six trades working here at one time. I've chosen paint, light fixtures, appliances, knobs, pulls, everything for the grandkids' new bath and bunkroom, carpet, tile, +++.

I've even bought some new furniture, a gorgeous area rug for my office, and stocked the kitchen and baths. We're still camping out with only a bed and folding table and chairs.

We've even managed to work on the business and attend some Homebuilder Association functions, a play and dinner with Scott and Liz. Talk about therapy - this is therapy for me and I am loving it! I just need to make sure I'm getting enough sleep and rest.

I talked to my oncologist in Austin yesterday. My biopsy results do show active growth, so now we are waiting for the genetic results to see if I can get into a trial, have immunotherapy, or ??? We'll see after the cyber knife treatments over the next month.

This week, I am so grateful for the fun I'm having in AR, for the beauty of this area, for evening boat rides with Howard (Ma and Pa Kettle go exploring), for creating another Owen family 'home', and for time spent with Scott, Liz, Carson, and Amelia.

Monday, we are flying to Camp Owen CO to spend time with Steven, Shannon, Westyn, Liam, and Brazos. Then after a few days of playing, movers will pack up one-half of everything in the CO house and head for Camp Owen Ozarks. The challenge is we need to leave the CO house staged for sale and livable for the family. H & I will return to AR on June 19 to supervise the unload.

Then, I'll come home to Austin for my cancer treatments. Exhausting, you say? YES, but I am very happy to be enjoying each day - and as long as I don't dwell on the past or on the future, I'm okay. One day at a time as a "maximizer." I have so much to live for. And that's my story today. Who knows what tomorrow may bring?

With love and gratitude,
Karen Sparky Strong

"Oh my, what a trip you had. But you have the power to turn everything into something good. I pray for you constantly and can't wait to hear about your next journey. You are totally an amazing human!"
Margi F

Happy Independence Day
fireworks and cyber knife radiation in Austin

"Beaver Lake!!! Love it.
Can't wait to visit.
Okay, so cyber knife is this month.
Okay! Jack and I can come meet you and
snuggle for an hour or so if you want?!!!
Let me know. Xo"
Jenny B Q

July 2, 2019

Hard to realize 2019 is half over. I truly can't believe how fast time is flying - and how busy I've been - on purpose. It was only five weeks ago we closed on our new/old lake house in AR.

Just prior to closing, Howard and I spent ten days in Camp Owen CO - with Steven, Shannon, and grandkids, and then moved almost half of the

CO furnishings to AR. As soon as we arrived in AR, we became immersed in the remodel and have worked at least ten hours each day supervising the transformation and finding new furniture and accessories to create our new Owen Lake Cottage overlooking the beautiful, pristine Beaver Lake, yet another of God's majestic, breathtaking creations.

This exciting endeavor has filled the hours while I've been waiting to start my cyber knife treatments. And tomorrow, Howard and I, with Barkley and Chollo, will head back to Austin for the holiday weekend. Then Howard will head right back to AR on Sunday.

I will stay in Austin for unusually super-intense cyber knife radiation treatments on July

9, 11, 15, 17, and 19. I can't wait to talk to my doctor to find out why he scheduled extra long treatments. Here's hoping for success: I'm planning to dodge the expected follow-up chemo.

I'm feeling so good that, other than sporadic pain and exhaustion (could it be from my daily activity level?), it's hard to believe those pesky cancer cells have invaded again. I am focusing on self-talk and meditation to enhance my own body's healing powers.

We all have an untapped self-healing power; I sure hope I can corral mine!

I am confident I will prevail!

Yet I take each day as it comes and continue to try not to look back or too far forward - easier said than done, but a lofty goal.

> Have a wonderful 4th of July! Love those fireworks!
> Karen Sparky Strong

> "Karen Sparky Strong, you are a wonder!!
> You continue to amaze me with your energy, focus, and drive.
> Although I'm not surprised (because that's who you are),
> I'm exhausted just looking at all you've accomplished!
> Sounds like a wonderful beginning to the next chapter,
> and I'm excited for you!
> Keep rockin' and rollin', keep up the positive attitude,
> and being present. You're always in my thoughts!
> Happy Independence Day!"
> Pam W

> "Yay! After the cyber knife treatments and
> all that beauty sleep, you'll be more awesome than ever!"
> Kathy R

PIECE OF CAKE
painless, easy, and uneventful treatment

"So very happy the procedure was not painful.
You've been through the ringer.
Prayers constantly coming your way!"
Ree O

July 9, 2019

After such a long delay, I finally had my first cyber knife radiation treatment today. This was the easiest, most painless, non-invasive, and uneventful medical treatment I've had in the last year-and-a-half. The predicted side effect is exhaustion, and I did come home and sleep for five hours.

But that's a small price to pay for potential eradication of my liver tumors. I have four more treatments over the next ten days, and then the pensive wait for results at my next CT scan in 45 days.

Thank you all for your thoughtful and supportive cards, calls, emails, and messages to help me through this next phase of this onerous cancer journey. I am absolutely confident that these cyber knife treatments will be successful and that I won't need to have chemo for the next year: that is my hope and prayer.

Time for more sleep!

With so much love and gratitude,
Karen Sparky Strong

"Karen, I continue to be so grateful for
what God can do when we go to him
AND when we try to help."
Jeani & Col. John

Back To The Beginning
tumors growing again - not in the game plan

"I have been keeping up with your news as you write it.
Thank you for being so open with your results.
I am praying for you, friend. Do not lose heart!
Trust God is with you as you walk out these very difficult days.
You are loved!"
Debbie C

July 12, 2019

Bad news. After my cyber knife treatment yesterday, I met with my radiation oncologist. He opened with, "I didn't want to have this discussion on the phone..."

My blood pressure rose, my heart rate accelerated, and I had an immediate hot flash - no, no, no. I didn't want to hear what I feared he would say.

Given the troubling view of my June MRI, scan results, and the glaring plethora of new tumors and growing 'old' tumors, Dr. Rivera ordered new blood work, an MRI, and a CT scan early next week, squeezed in between my cyber knife treatments and an appointment with my primary oncologist to determine what broad spectrum regimen I will need to begin asap.

This new news is every cancer's patient's worst fear. I'm trying to wrap my head around my new reality, and I'm really struggling. Dr. Rivera said I need to get back on my very strict cancer diet, resume intense meditation, etc., etc., etc.

Sigh. All of this really requires a mental reset, especially if Dr. Shimkus finds there are no treatments other than chemo. The reality of the limited cures for pancreatic cancer is hitting pretty hard.

I'll pull out all the stops again. I've already reached out to MD Anderson for a second opinion from my pancreatic oncologist, Dr. Javle. I sure hope I hear back from him very soon.

Needless to say, Howard, my kids, and our close friends are as upset as I am. I'm sure I'll feel better a week from now when we have a new plan. I hadn't considered this scenario, and I'm resistant to going back to February 2018 when my life changed with the onset of my cancer and I pushed through for the first time. Here I go again. And I'm trying to focus on my earned name: Karen Sparky Strong.

Please ratchet up your prayers and support. I need you now more than ever.

More to come,
Karen

"So many thoughts going through my head…
most of them starting with 'f$&k'!
My heart and soul are with you from New Jersey.
Tell me what you need me to do and it is yours!"
Martha V

"Rats! None us out here in cyberspace wanted to hear that.
Prayers will be even harder and longer for you, Sparky!"
Marion M

"Karen Strong: We can only imagine how discouraging
this news is. BUT you are truly a force of nature,
with incredible inner resolve and strength,
who inspires all who are fortunate be in your presence.
We are sending positive thoughts, prayers, hugs & love.
Thank you for your inspiration and bravery,
and for sharing your journey."
Lynn T

JUST THE FACTS
back on the monster fulfirinox

"Your future fight is incomprehensible.,
but your friends are sending all support possible.
You are a treasure."
Nancy McC

July 18, 2019

- I have so much gratitude for all your love and support, which means more to me than you'll ever realize.
- I've just seen my primary oncologist.
- Results of Tuesday's tests show aggressive growth of new and old tumors in my liver.
- I will start six months of Fulfirinox (the monster of chemos) next week because this is the chemo I was on the first time, which yielded such good results. This means I'm facing everything I 'survived' last February through July all over again. And, I'll lose my new beautiful blond hair…
- I will finish my first round of cyber knife radiation tomorrow, and then I will begin another round to treat the largest of my liver tumors.

No commentary today… just wanted to respond to so many of your caring inquiries.

Love,
KO

"Karen Strong, you've got this!
Think of the first go 'round as practice and you aced it!
It's not back to square 1, it's "I've done this before,
and I can do it again because I'm a fighter, and I'm Karen Strong!!!"
Sending lots of hugs and positive thoughts!"
Pam W

Just the facts, ma'am:
(with apologies to Sgt. Joe Friday,
for those of us old enough to remember *Dragnet*):

1. This is news no one wanted to hear, most of all you.

2. Your friends and family will double down with love and prayers.

3. You have given a gift to everyone with whom you shared this news. You set an example of how to go through a tough diagnosis and treatment.

4. There is much cause for optimism, as your body responded so well to this before. And with each month, new cures and studies are emerging.

5. Hair grows back.

Kathy R

"I like the idea of your friends and family
'doubling down' on you, Karen.
Prayers and good vibes to the max.
We are all strong together. XOXOX"
Trudy McC

"Just the facts:
you got this!
you are loved!
you are Karen Strong!"
Jane B

Gotta Do What I Gotta Do
I WILL WIN the Fulfirinox battle

"Round 2 and you are as strong as ever!
Remember you have TEAM KAREN behind you!
Much love!"
Rosemary L

July 29, 2019

Today is that dreaded Monday, but I am now comfortably ensconced in a leather La-Z-Boy chair in the infusion lab wrapped in a blanket while four bags of my Fulfirinox cocktail drip into my body through the port. Six hours today, and I'm four hours in. My memory senses are on red alert—the whooziness , sleepiness, imbalance, over-sensitized taste buds have already returned—and that's in the first few hours.

I'll go home later today with an external pump which will continue to feed the healing 'poison' into my body for 48 more hours. Tomorrow I will start my second round of five more cyber knife radiation treatments over the next two weeks. And at the same time, I'll get my pump removed Wednesday and then follow up Thursday and Friday with shots to regrow and boost my white blood cell count.

And the beat goes on and on and on…

I must admit, I was very 'down' Saturday when Howard and I drove back to Austin. We arrived home late and dragged nine days' worth of mail into the house. As I sorted the mail, I was touched by the huge stack of beautiful, loving cards I had received while we were in Arkansas.

I always read every card (as well as every note, text, email, FB comment, VM, +++). Your prayers, encouragement, love, positive comments, and devotionals lifted me. With your pervasive support, I wrapped my head around so many loving friends and family who are encouraging me: I gratefully accept your gifts, and in that process, I decided to *Just Do It* - again.

Today, I started climbing the second big chemo/radiation mountain with Howard by my side. Please know that YOU are part of me on this journey, so don't abandon me now!

We had been in AR for nine days while waiting for this new chapter to begin. We had such a great time working to make the AR lake house a home. I guilted Howard into helping me hang heavy, high pictures, assemble headboards, and even vacuum.

The painters are still there, the iron railings and backsplash tiles need to be installed, etc., but when we get back to AR, we should be very close to 'finished' - the whole remodel completed in the record time of 2.5 months thanks to our son SCOTT, who strongly encouraged his subs to work on our house.

Last week, I spent hours in the recliner on the screened porch peacefully looking at the lake - great therapy and calm. Looking forward to getting back there and doing more of the same.

With love and gratitude,
Karen

"Sweet Karen, You are such a warrior
and a role model for many who follow your path.
Stay strong and know you have many pom-poms
waving high in the air cheering you on.
Sending lots of love and hugs."
Patti H

"Continued prayers to the Big Guy upstairs,
may He grant you peace of mind and strength to fight this fight,
give you hope for a cure, and help you keep your faith.
Keep trusting in Him while you continue to be Karen Strong."
Gigi R

ONE WEEK DOWN
double whammy takes its toll

"You did it!! Amazing job!!
Keep up the great work. Focus on the victories!!
The less you worry and stress, the faster your body
will heal... easier said than done.
But you are a superwoman and a continued survivor... xoxo"
Courtney R

August 3, 2019

I did it! I survived a week of BOTH chemo and cyber knife radiation.

What does that look like? Well, this week alone, I absorbed six hours of chemo infusions at the lab, 46 hours of additional chemo pumped into my port, four hours of cyber knife radiation, blood tests, and two shots to help rebuild my white blood cell count.

And when Howard and I weren't circling the city for doctor appointments and treatments, I was sleeping. The doctors told me this double whammy would wipe me out - and it DID! I've never slept so much or been so lazy in my entire life.

However, from the chemo, I'm already having side effects I had forgotten about: the blisters in my mouth are beyond painful and irritating, I'm back to eating just for nutrition, because nothing tastes good, plus touching or drinking anything cold is like getting an electric shock, and I'm pretty slow movin'.

This upcoming week should be better. I only have three sessions of cyber knife. I'll be wiped out again, but surely I'll have more energy than this past week.

I must admit, I am so lucky to have such beautiful homes for recovery. In Austin, I spend hours floating in our pool, surrounded by our wildflower garden and greenery. In Arkansas, the view of the lake from our deck provides unlimited water therapy, calm, and peace.

And as Howard says, 'There was nowhere better on earth to commune with God than sitting on our CO deck, praising His majestic mountainous creation."

We'll be returning to AR next Saturday and stay there until November. I'll get my chemo treatments at Highlands Oncology in Fayetteville and Rogers. In September, we'll fly from AR to Houston for my consultation at MD Anderson. Here's hoping Dr. Javle has some new tricks up his sleeve.

I'm pulling out all the stops to scuttle those fast-growing, rebellious cancer cells. I only hope it is God's plan that I still have more work to do on this earth because I intend to be here for awhile.

That said, I know your prayers will be heard, so please keep them shooting straight into the lap of God.

Always with love and gratitude,
Karen

PS. If any of you plan to be in Northwest Arkansas over the next several months, PLEASE come and visit us. Just say when and our door will be open.   Love, K

"You just amaze me, Karen, with your positive attitude.
Please know I am praying for you and
God's wonderful plan he has for you.
You are such an inspiration to everyone.
Hang in there and know you have lots of cheerleaders!! XO"
Denise H

"Karen, I love your positiviness (is that a word?)
and resolve. Will be in AR in a couple weeks
and will stop and get/give a hug."
Susan W

MORE THAN A WEEK'S REPRIEVE
cyber knife machine takes a vacation

"Wow, Karen, you are a warrior!
I am praying for you each day and
know God is watching over you.
Sending you lots of love."
Leigh H

August 12, 2019

I was scheduled to finish my cyber knife treatments last week. Lo and behold, the radiation monster broke!

I spent the week sleeping, being lazy, and waiting for the big news that the machine was repaired: just got news that today is the day.

It's Monday morning and I'm all mentally geared up for this weeks' onslaught: currently sitting in the big leather recliner in the infusion lab, writing my journal, but... my nurse just told me my white cell count is sooo low, I can't get treated.

Geez, given that I had a week off, this is bad news. No wonder I slept and slept and slept through the days and nights last week (actually, the last 2½ weeks).

I'm now getting another series of shots over the next three days, so I hope we can do chemo next week. There go our plans for AR. Who knows when we'll get up there now. I'll do chemo in Austin next week and then we'll see...

Just left the chemo lab and am heading to cyber knife radiation.

Pushing through,
K

"We are hoping the harder the journey (yours certainly is)
the bigger the rewards... we love you!"
Jeani & Col. John

Back To Bald... And To Arkansas
round two of baldness

"You are beautiful with or without hair!
Have a wonderful time with your family!"
Cindy J

August 29, 2019

I am filled with loving kindness.
I feel good!!!!
I am peaceful and at ease.
I am Happy!!!
I am experiencing Total Health NOW!!
Thank you, Father!!

I am sitting in the screened porch at our lake house overlooking Beaver Lake, AR. It is a beautiful day, I feel good, and I wanted to share some of my common daily affirmations (above). I'm more convicted on some days than others, but I am a firm believer in the power of positive thinking.

The last several weeks have been challenging, but I've come out on the good side just in time for the family to join Howard and me in AR for Labor Day, and for the grandkids to discover Owen Lake Cottage. I can't wait!

I finished cyber knife radiation treatments in Austin three weeks ago. During treatment, I discovered how fortunate I am to live in Austin where there is a cyber knife machine. There are only five in Texas and about 30 nationally.

Then two weeks ago (after five Zarzio shots), my blood cell count was high enough to get my newly 25% reduced dose Fulfirinox chemo cocktail.

Last weekend, we were able to come back to AR, where we'll probably stay until October-November.

But before we left, my hair was falling out, so Tiffany and I visited a salon: Tiffany got a haircut and I had my head shaved. It's amazing, but

Howard now prefers me *au naturel* rather than wearing wigs or scarves, so the new me does serious eye makeup, bright lipstick, big earrings, and an 'attitude.' Given that Texas has suffered through a heat wave of 100°+ for weeks, bald sure is cooler!

I met with my new AR oncologist last Monday; he will be managing my chemo treatments while we're here. The good news: Dr. Beck (AR) is in total agreement with the treatment plan proposed by Dr. Shimkus (TX), and Dr. Beck also proposed a visit to MD Anderson (already scheduled). Why?

I've received the results of my gene study, and I have a gene mutation identified as HER1. This mutation causes unstoppable tumor growth and can't be turned off. There is a treatment for this mutation, but the treatment is only approved by the FDA for breast cancer and gastro-intestinal cancer - and NOT for pancreatic cancer.

When I go back to MD Anderson, we will discover if my current treatments are 'working.' If they are, we'll continue with current chemo until January. If not, I will try to get into a trial asap to shut off my mutant gene.

Meanwhile I'm back to trying to live one day at a time: not back or forward - but living in the present and being thankful for each and every day. (Easier said than done!)

Today and tomorrow, I'm scurrying around hanging curtains, making new beds with new linens, grocery shopping, +++: awaiting the family's arrival.

Have a great Labor Day weekend!

xoxo,
Karen

"New home sweet home for a healing touch.
I totally agree with Howard on the natural look!"
Judy W

"You know if you say "bald" and "Arkansas" really fast 10 times,
it begins to sound like BadAss! Just sayin'."
Kathy R

SOME LABOR DAY WEEKENDS ARE BETTER THAN OTHERS...
Kids & grandkids make for a super holiday weekend

"OH MY GOSH!
You really need to have a reality TV show.
And once again you have endured with style and grace
(yes, I am picturing you crawling on hands and knees)
You are beyond amazing. I hope you heal quickly. Love you."
Kathy G

September 2, 20198

FRIDAY - I felt good, but anxious, as we tracked Shannon on her nine-hour solo drive with Westyn (7), Liam (4) and Brazos (2) from Austin to Owen Lake Cottage. She sloshed through three hours of monsoon rains and a one-hour accident delay, which extended her whole trip to twelve hours - ugh.

Friday evening, Scott (with Carson (4) and Amelia (2)), picked Steven up from the airport, since he had flown in from a business trip to Cincinnati. Finally, they all arrived (sans Liz who is in the middle of staging our new Model) for the Labor Day weekend.

What an auspicious beginning! The grandkids love their new bunkroom/bath on the third floor. My ultimate compliment was that our kids like this house as well as Camp Owen CO. Now, that's saying something!

SATURDAY - A beautiful sunny sunrise with cool temps. First favorite on the agenda: ATV rides with Dads and Papa, playing in the yard with ropes, riding toys, little monster trucks, and fly swatters (yes, you read right - great for four-year-old non-lethal sword fights.)

Next, lunch and naps FOR ALL. And then we were ready for the big boating afternoon with the super-duper tow float Nana bought, so the grandkids can ride the waves. On to the lake and into the water.

In my zeal sorting through ropes, life jackets, towels, food, drinks, +++ for the ten of us (good thing we bought a big boat up here), I pulled a tangled mess of ropes out of a fore storage container. Little did I know, Howard had removed the cover to the huge hull storage container; I stepped backwards and free-fell into the hull. OH, such pain and shock.

I am so fortunate I didn't break my back or neck or get a huge concussion. Alas, after Steven and Scott hauled me out and assessed my condition, I emerged with only a HUGE colorful bruise on my derriere (TMI) and a very sore and swollen foot. Onward we went for an adventurous and enjoyable boating excursion. And Liz was able to join us later.

SUNDAY - I awoke with elephantiasis of my right foot. But being Karen Strong, I was still limping around hanging the new tree swing when my daughters-in-law took one look at my foot and dictated an imminent visit to the emergency room.

Several hours later, I emerged with crutches and two broken bones in my foot wrapped securely in a hard splint, with directions to get to an orthopaedist Thursday to get my cast. The ER docs had quickly assessed that a cancer/chemo patient cannot do surgery - too much risk of infection, bones too brittle, immune system too compromised.

The issue here is it is a holiday and I am on crutches; chemo patients have weak arm and leg strength and a compromised sense of balance. How well do you think I'm doing on crutches? I can't even lift myself up a step, so I crawled on hands and knees to get in the house.

THIS is not a pretty picture

I've even abandoned my affirmations for the time being. To add insult to injury, we can't get a scooter until Tuesday when I go to town for my chemo infusions.

I need to be off my foot, keep it elevated and iced, and wait for the swelling to go down. Combine that with the side effects of chemo this week, and I think I'm in for "it."

MONDAY -The kids and grandkids left this morning. The grandkids had a great time but were quite miffed when Nana couldn't get out of the La-Z-Boy chair. I'm miffed, too, although so grateful I wasn't hurt worse. But come on, I don't need to be in a cast for two months. I sure will be glad when:

1) I can sit down without excruciating pain

2) I can get in the hot tub again

3) I can drive again (yes, my right foot)

4) I get my scooter

5) I'm ready for more affirmations

My bucket (not cup) runneth over - when will it stop?

In the interim, watch for KO-kamikaze on her new scooter. And no laughing when you visualize me climbing stairs on my hands and knees. That's the only way I'll be able to get on the first and third floors of my house.

> With love, gratitude, and angst,
> KO-kamikaze

> "My mouth is wide open
> and the '7 dirty words you can't say on television'
> re: George Carlin (now you can say them)
> ARE coming out of my mouth. You fell in the fricking Hull.
> OK - deep breath. You will heal and the pain will get better.
> This is just a bump in the road.
> Is this what it takes to get you to rest?????
> I wish you healing thoughts and easy chemo coming up.
> Take care. Please."
> Judy W

> "OMG!! So sorry this happened & you're all right!!
> Careful, you might get a speeding ticket on your scooter.
> Ever the amazing trooper, swollen foot & major bruises
> did not slow you down. Hope swelling & bruising goes away soon."
> Lynn T

@#$%^&!
bummer

September 3, 2019

I awoke this morning psychologically geared up for another chemo day.

Inch by inch, I pulled my sore and weary body out of bed on those dangerous, clumsy crutches. (Remember, chemo patients have compromised balance.) The blisters on my palms and the sore arms/pits spoke to me, as did my big, blue-black bruise and swollen foot.

Howard poured me into the car and we headed to Highlands Oncology for chemo. Upon arrival, the nurses informed me last week's blood results didn't look good, so we had to redo blood work.

Twenty minutes later, doctor's message: "White blood cell count and platelets too low to get chemo. Reschedule for next week and take three Zarzio shots today, tomorrow, and Thursday. Come back tomorrow for an IV infusion. Eat lots and lots of protein. Immunities VERY low - stay away from public places and germs."

Scott plans to give me a rolling office chair to use until my rolling knee scooter arrives Thursday - much better than crutches. Howard continues to support my every need, but now agrees that I'm pretty helpless.

Seeing orthopaedist tomorrow. Fingers crossed. Toes still look like sausages.

Feeling pretty bummed. But tomorrow is only a day away.

Sleep well,
KO

A Day For Good News
finally free

"GREAT news!!
So glad to hear your foot is healing and
you can get around again.
Should have known there is no stopping you.
Good luck with the opening- an exciting time for you."
Peggy H

September 10, 2019

I'm free! *I'm free!*

Well, SOMEWHAT free. After chemo today, (Yes, my counts were FINALLY high enough to get my infusion today - YAY!) I went directly to my appointment with the orthopaedic. He set me freer. No more wheelchair, no more knee scooter: just a walking boot and a cane, with orders to limit activities that put strain on my knee and foot, since I'll be in this boot for 4+ months.

Oh, and he gave me a cortisone shot and anti-inflammatories to mitigate the tendonitis, arthritis, and fluid build-up in my knee caused by the knee scooter. I had used a knee walker years ago when I had foot surgery and it was a Godsend. I did not realize that cancer/chemo have debilitated my bones, muscles, and tendons 'til they are super-sensitive to any pressure/invasion.

When I got the walker last week, it served to damage my knee. Now I have progressed from Thundering Snail (on the rolling office chair) to Speedy (on the knee walker) to Peg Leg (in the boot). With time and practice, who knows what Howard will call me next!

He also feels he has been set free: he has been my major domo, butler, housekeeper, personal servant, and shoulder to cry on, all with his full-time role developing Sapphire Homes with Scott. I'm not sure which of us is happier tonight.

Tomorrow morning, we will meet with my AR oncologist to ascertain if he will add the new protocols recommended by my Austin oncologist. Fingers crossed. And then we'll head to MD Anderson in two weeks: that will be a very important results week.

In the interim, A FULL schedule ahead as we have the Grand Opening of our MODEL home in Averie Estates this Thursday night. Then lots of family coming to see our new digs here in Eureka Springs. My immediate hope and prayer is that my chemo side effects are minimal and that my pancreatic oncologist at MD Anderson has good news for me...

Love, Love, Love your texts, cards, emails, comments, phone calls. You have no idea how much your support and prayers have meant to me during this past very challenging month. Counting on good things and good news in the coming month. Onward and upward!

With love and gratitude,
Peg Leg

"Averie Estates... choked me up. Beautiful, Karen."
Barbara N

"Good news, Peg Leg, you are up mobile and on the go!
Good luck with the Averie Opening!
Prayers for good news from the MD Anderson oncologist."
Cindy W

"Very good news.
Moving forward in a very positive direction.
Please behave yourself!"
Judy W

THE GOOD, THE BAD, AND THE HOPEFUL
back to MD Anderson

"Ugh. The frustration y'all must've felt.
Prayers continuing plus prayers that ALL the information
is there for you. YOU are amazing. Stay strong"
Janet M

September 26, 2019

This is the day I've been waiting for: my visit to MD Anderson to ascertain the results of recent months of cyber knife radiation and Fulfirinox chemo. Dr. Javle came into the patient room... and the ceiling fell in. He had not received ANY of the records from either my Austin or AR oncologists.

In the end, it doesn't matter where in the chain the files got waylaid. All that matters is that Dr. Javle didn't have the relevant data for comparison; he didn't have the CT scan CDs from the last four months of CDs to evaluate if I'm getting better or worse; he didn't have the latest CARIS Gene Study results that identify my out-of-control gene mutation. All he had was ME and the lab work and CT scan results from yesterday.

What did we learn?

• My pancreatic tumor that started all this chaos and disappeared last October has come back and is growing – BAD news.
• My liver tumors that reared their ugly little heads in May are still thriving – BAD news.
• I still have NO pain and Dr. Javle says I look healthy – a BIG deal for cancer patients – GOOD news.
• Dr. wants to see the results of my most recent Gene Study to further understand that pesky gene mutation. My mutated gene was not present in the first gene study a year ago – very strange. If it is what he thinks it is, he wants to treat me with a different treatment cocktail. The treatment (whose name I can't remember) has not shown to be very successful for pancreatic

cancer patients, but Dr. Javle said it will be worth trying – HOPEFUL news.

• If after he receives all my medical data the Fulfirinox chemo doesn't prove successful, he will shift me to the one other chemo cocktail available for pancreatic cancer patients - HOPEFUL news.

My job now is to get my hands on ALL the test results and CDs from the plethora of tests I've had since May, and to FedEx them to Dr. Javle. We will then schedule a conference call and he will roll out his recommendations for my immediate future BASED ON MY DATA. Need I add that Dr. Javle, Howard, and I are all beyond frustrated? It will now be two more weeks until we have concrete answers and a plan of action.

After our disappointing consultation, Howard and I jumped in a service car bound for Bush International airport, and just landed in Northwest AR. GOOD news: the weather is absolutely beautiful here, Howard's brother, sister-in-law, and sister arrive tomorrow, and we're looking forward to another fun weekend.

For now, I'm getting all my ducks in a row and plan to have this figured out in a week to ten days.

Another positive: Howard and I had dinner last night with an 'old' friend (and her husband), who had started teaching with me at Murchison Junior High in Austin in 1972. We haven't seen each other in about ten years, so what a great evening! Oh, the stories we told from 47 years ago! Gulp.

Back to today: I must admit, I was in tears as we left Houston earlier this afternoon, but I'm regaining my equilibrium, and will probably feel better after a good night's sleep. (I haven't been sleeping well since before the second anniversary of Blake's passing.)

I am overwhelmed with all your prayers and best wishes for great results today. Well, it didn't work out the way I had hoped, but that means you are NOT off the hook: I am requesting at least another two weeks of prayers and support. I can't make my tumors shrink or disappear, so "Lord, hear our prayers."

With love and gratitude – mixed with a sprinkling of frustration, angst, and fear,

Peg Leg (for 3 more months – ugh)

"What a disappointing day and YET,
you find good!!
You will always be an inspiration in my life!!
God is surrounding you with his love."
Denise H

LOVING THE FALL TEMPS OF AR
beautiful fall AR foliage,
not so pretty pancreatic tumors

October 11, 2019

Loving the overnight shift in temperatures - from the 90s to the 40s. Isn't it invigorating? Now we're waiting for our first glorious change of leaves in AR...

Just glad I'm not in Denver or the NE - not ready for freezes or snow. We're still in AR, but will return to Austin mid-next week.

We have had oodles of company and had sooo much fun with everyone. But I will admit, it took 16 hours of sleep yesterday to bring me back to 'functionality.'

And Tiffany is still here. What a wonderful gift for the two of us to have this relaxing, mother-daughter time together (which rarely happens).

During the last week, I have talked to two of my oncologists who have been able to compare my July scans with the most recent September scans from MDA. Overall, a mixed report.

The cyber knife radiation was not as successful as hoped, but my cyber knife oncologist said the effects can take up to six months, so I'm asking Santa for total obliteration of those radiated tumors for Christmas.

The other new, small liver tumors have not shown any shrinkage YET, so full forward with Fulfirinox for the full months. My pancreatic tumor has reared its ugly head again, providing a second reason to continue with broad spectrum chemo.

And last but not least, there is a new small spot on my lung that we will be watching closely. In summary, on a scale of 1-5, I was at a 3 last July, and now a 2.5. So onward, onward, onward.

Will be back in Austin for my next chemo treatment, and still waiting to talk to my MDA oncologist. The next big question is how to deal with my gene mutation, which is the genesis of my tumor growth. Next phase? TBD...

Off to Eureka Springs with Tiffany.

With love and gratitude,
Karen Strong

"Invigorating!! That's the adjective I've been looking for!
I've been saying crisp and clean. I love it, too.
Good to hear all the good stuff. Keep it up, Mama! Love you guys!"
Jenny B Q

"Writing a letter to a Santa in your name!!!!
Love you."
Jeani & Col. John

Bump, Bump, Bump on This Winding Road
mondays becoming hump days

"Each day I pray that one of these treatments will be effective.
If only they can come up with an immune treatment for P C.
Love you and keep fighting. Last year at this time
you and Howard were out here and the fall colors
were very dull and brown and this year they are radiant.
Love you and hang in there."
Jeanne C

October 21, 2019

Mondays are turning out to be hump days for me.

Remember in college, we called Wednesdays 'Hump Day' because we were two days away from Fun Fridays and it gave us a semi-legit reason to party mid-week. I don't know why I thought of that (so many years ago) because Mondays are turning out to be my Hump Days for a very different reason. Most Mondays now, I'm getting blood work and cyber knife radiation or chemo.

And believe me, I'm not partying!

Today is one of the bumpiest days I can recall. It started with blood work followed by an appointment with my Austin oncologist, Dr. Shimkus. This was the first time I've talked to him since he received my CT scan results from MD Anderson and has had my comparative results from May through October.

Today was my reveal non-party to hear his go forward plan, and I sure don't like what he had to say. I've been processing all afternoon.

In summary, my current Fulfirinox treatment is NOT slowing my tumor growth, and we already knew that the cyber knife results are mixed and sub-optimal. He recommended I get my final Fulfirinox chemo infusion today (which I did, and now have my external pump until Wednesday, when the pump is disconnected. Then I will get my Neulasta pump to rebuild my white blood cells). He wants to get ahead of rapid tumor growth before it gets that bad.

Right now, the tumor growth is slow, but he doesn't expect that to last. So attack, attack, attack.

When I see Dr. Shimkus next Monday (my new Hump Day), we will start over with a completely new chemo treatment called Taxal/Gemstar. It is an alternative pancreatic chemo treatment, but it is considered a secondary level infusion treatment. Fulfirinox is the only primary for pancreatic cancer, and we'll have to "Just Do It" to see if it works for me.

We will start at full potency every two weeks and see what the side effects and results will be. Brian (Dr. S) also wants me to see if I can get into a trial at MDA, explore an ongoing trial currently running at my Oncology group in AR, or another pancreatic trial at Mass General. We hope the trials will focus on shutting down my HER2 gene mutation (Hopeful and early thinking).

So I've called my research analyst, our son Steven, back into active duty and have faith with his help, we will find a trial that can help me. I'm also enlisting the help of my Guardian Angel, Blake... and praying hard.

All of our plans for November and December will change, based on next Monday's doctor appointment in Austin. Howard was supposed to go back to AR today and I am supposed to go back this Friday. All bets are off as to when we go back to AR until after next Monday's new treatment plan.

I do know I'll be in Austin more than expected, and Howard will need to be in AR. Just taking it a day at a time for the foreseeable future. I do hope we'll get to CO for Christmas .

As I sit in my comfortable La-Z-Boy chair overlooking our pool at home in Austin on this glorious fall day, I'm feeling hope and mindfulness. I see my therapist tomorrow in my quest for a mind reset. It is going to take everything I have to plough through the bumps ahead on this new journey. As my oncology nurse said this morning, "Karen, fight, fight, fight."

And I WILL.

Please keep praying!

> With ongoing love and gratitude,
> Karen So Tired Strong

"Your strength and bold determination to fight
this fight with such grace is inspiring. You are a beautiful person.
Love your enthusiasm, joyful personality, and warm,
generous smile and laughter.
Praying for you everyday... for healing, strength, and peace."
Donna H

SOME WEEKS SEEM TO
LAST FOREVER
laying of the hands miraculous

"The experience you had at your Bible study brought me to tears.
I'm so thankful that grace came for you in your time of need
under the hands of loving friends.
Wishing you comfort and strength in the coming days."
Jacquetta

October 28, 2019

Time is so relative: some days seem to drag on forever and others whip by in seconds. Though I know seven days = seven days, I'm sure last week took seven weeks out of my life. And during that time, some 'things' happened that really rocked my world.

A week ago Monday, I swallowed the bad chemo news and spent the following several days spiraling down the vortex of ambiguity, depression, and fear, while trying to get some answers from my MD Anderson pancreatic oncologist on next steps and trials. During this same slippery slope, we scheduled Howard's upcoming knee replacement and his cataract surgery. Plus we are still grappling with containing his diabetes (next trip to the endocrinologist).

We were supposed to have returned to AR, but couldn't and didn't. By Wednesday night, my emotions took control and I just lost it. I've been praying and trying to put my trust in the Lord, and so many of you have been praying for me.

Why wasn't I feeling God's love, grace, or healing?

Then Thursday morning, despite my emotional and psychological drought, I decided to go to my Bible study group (since I was still in Austin anyway), but I was in such a weakened state, I also intended to just listen - not share.

As our discussion progressed, I kept thinking, *why am I here?* I don't want to 'unload' on this group.

And then it happened: I just starting sobbing and spewing what was in my heart, including how difficult it had been to survive both Averie's and Blake's recent anniversaries on top of my latest chemo news, struggles to get doctor info, which would help us make the best decision for extending my life, etc., etc., etc.

THEN IT HAPPENED.

Every friend in my Bible study group laid her hands on me, called upon God, prayed for me, and cried with me. I've never felt an intensity, connectedness, or power like it. And it was at that moment I felt new peace, calm, and hope in my soul.

At that very moment, I knew Jesus had not abandoned me, that with His help I will persevere, and I will find joy in living each day that will carry me through to whatever is God's plan for me (easier said than done).

I drove directly to the doctor's office after Bible study and dealt with yet more complications, but it was okay, since I was getting back on track. In fact, Thursday night, we were at Dance Club with dear friends - and Howard (with his bad knee) and I (with my booted broken foot) hobbled gingerly to our favorites.

And the best? I led the LaBamba line dance around the floor in my medical boot, black Halloween stretch pants, AND my new sassy wig! A turnabout in six hours! Miracles do happen.

Now what?

After putting all the puzzle pieces together (just this morning):

1) I'm going to start the new chemo treatments on Nov. 11.

2) We're going to appeal to the insurance company to cover a drug that is very expensive, yet not covered (prayers needed).

3) In a few weeks, I'm going for testing to see if I qualify for a trial at MDA to address my gene mutation Positive HER2. However, this will be a last resort, as this trial is a Phase 1 First-in-Human trial - more info to come before I put my eggs in this basket.

I'm so glad it is Monday again and we had a solid discussion with Dr. Shimkus this morning. At least we have a plan...

I know, I know. This journal entry has been rather unusual, but I truly experienced how the Lord can work in mysterious ways, and not just for me but for all of us as we face life's bumps in the road.

We're off to AR tomorrow for a quick trip before we return to Austin to deal with all our medical issues. But we're not like our other senior citizen friends who get together and discuss aches, pains, meds, and our young surgeons/professionals who were in our carpools when they went to school with our kids.

NO, I'm not like that. *I'm worse.*

DOING THE HAPPY DANCE...
SANS MEDICAL BOOT!
Dr. Beck (HOG) works a deal with Genentech

"Happy dancing right with you, lady!
Hugs, love and prayers continuing!"
Rachel K

November 4, 2019

It must be Monday again. It seems as though I communicate with doctors and their staffs all week long, wait through the weekend, and then get the answers to my questions the following Monday.

Today is a big day. Why?

Prior to my return to AR, Dr. Shimkus (in Austin) said he wanted to change my chemo regimen and would check with insurance to see if they would cover the drug (not likely) that would address my positive HER2 gene mutation. Since then, we confirmed insurance would not pay and that the cost could be ~$3K per week.

When we got back to AR, I went to see Dr. Beck (my oncologist at Highland Oncology Group). He was able to petition Genentech, and they are going to provide my gene therapy meds FREE.

(Excited about taking more cancer drugs? Hmm, everything is relative and I now feel very blessed. My insurance denial also brings our entire medical insurance issues to the forefront.)

Our hope is these new gene drugs decimate the gene mutation that causes tumor growth. Or at least, this is what I've been able to piece together. (I think I'll be continuing Fulfirinox, but it could change to Gemzar/Abraxane. And the gene protocol is Herceptin and Pertuzamab. (So confusing, but at least I take good notes.)

We returned to AR last Tuesday, and on Wednesday I did blood work and a CT scan in prep for the new protocol. Much to my surprise, Dr. Beck called me Thursday afternoon and said my CT results looked pretty good. Most tumors have shrunk - some even 50%, all since September.

God is good.

The adventure continues: I will discover this Wednesday what my treatment schedule will be for the next few months. We'll probably be in AR most of the time except for Thanksgiving and Christmas in Austin. Yep, that means no Christmas in CO with the kids and grandkids, but I am going to have that discussion with Dr. Beck this week, too.

I can hardly imagine missing family Christmas in CO, but between my chemo and Howard's knee replacement, it may not be in the cards this year - though I haven't given up yet.

We returned just in time for the beautiful fall foliage and even took a leisurely boat ride on our glistening Beaver Lake yesterday. Today, I took my first walk in two matching shoes (sans medical boot) since Labor Day, when I broke my foot. What a great day!

What a difference a week can make. Will let you know what happens Wednesday...

Doing the happy dance without my boot today!
Karen

"One word for this entry: WOW!"
Mark K

"I am also doing a happy dance for you
about your tumor is shrinking!
You are the definition in the dictionary that says 'Survivor'."
Bonnie F

"So happy to hear the good news, sweet girl!
Love your enthusiasm and zest for life!!!
Am doing the happy dance with you!
Praying for you everyday."
Donna H

Godwinks In Abundance!
read godwink stories

" I love your Godwink story!!
It's so encouraging and amazing to see how God has had
His hand on you and provided for you during this journey.
I can't wait to see more Godwinks!!
You are such an inspiration to me and to many!!
Prayers continue for you, my friend. XOXO"
Mary D

November 6, 2019

I'm reading a fascinating devotional called *Godwink Stories*. 'Godwinks' are the so-called coincidences we would normally dismiss that in fact do mean something. And we need to pay attention and recognize them. They are like unopened gifts that have been placed on our doorstep.

My 'Godwinks' are proof that God does have a plan for me and that he really is a part of my everyday life. I'd like to share the culmination of a BIG Godwink that I am so grateful for today.

As you know, I've been struggling since late September to uncover and decide all my future options given the mixed CT results from MD Anderson in September. It took until last week (and lots of questions and perseverance) to discover that Dr. Beck in AR (not Austin or MDA) would provide the gene mutation drugs I need at no cost to me; in Austin it was $2.5K per week.

Today I learned Dr. Beck led the Herpicin-Perjeta trial with Genentech that was successful enough for him to be written up in the *New England Journal of Medicine* as co-author. (The trial is closed and data is in analytics.) AND, there were no pancreatic cancer patients in the trial, so Genentech and Dr. Beck are giving me the drug as their first pancreatic patient to test - with great hope that I will be their breakthrough patient.

Is that not a Godwink that we are even in AR to start a business, that Liz found me this recommended Oncologist in Rogers AR, that I chose to be treated up here too, that this doctor "owns" the key to med I need, and that they will still give me the drug post-trial (rare)?

This is a BIG Godwink in my book! Running down this winding path on my journey...

Back to today: VERY exciting appointment with Dr. Beck as we have scheduled all my appointments/treatments through January. We will be home in Austin two weeks for Thanksgiving.

AND biggest news of all: we're going to COLORADO for CHRISTMAS. Dates TBD.

Today, I had an echocardiogram and blood work, and then completed 4.5 hours of my 10.5 hour infusions protocol. I'll return at 7:45 AM for the remaining 6.5 hours of infusions followed by my two-day external pump and immune rescue shots.

Overwhelming? Yes, but so grateful to be receiving the best on today's market for me! And maybe my success will help others pancreatic patients in the future.

As I recollected the past two troubling months, I've identified many 'Godwinks' that I didn't understand until today. But this is helping me understand that God does have a plan for me - I just hope and pray it continues to be a positive one. And maybe someday He'll share why Blake and why Averie.

I'll be looking for more Godwinks in the interim.

With love and gratitude,
Karen Sparky Strong

"This is a Double Wink update.
Keep the positive news flowing.
Dr. Beck needs a customized cape... he is the man!"
Courtney R

"LOVE the Godwinks. Karen, YOU are a Godwink to all of us.
You are loved and admired by soooo many!"
Marion M

"Grab those Godwinks with both hands. Never let go."
Mary C

Double Whammy
Takes Its Toll
hard work and determination
to survive dual treatments

"Grandchildren are so precious!
Wishing you a healthy and strong Thanksgiving -
want you to feel good and enjoy each moment with family!!
Thinking of you each day with love."
Carol C

November 21, 2019

Be careful what you wish for.

Howard and I have stayed in AR so I can receive my new gene therapy-FREE. (Thanks to Dr. Beck! He has referred to me as his 'trial of 1' - so we have high hopes for positive results.)

My first double whammy was two weeks ago. Oh my goodness! It has been a tough two weeks.

Early last week I caught a bad cold, which coincided with a week of the worst side effects I've experienced in 1½ years of cancer treatments. By last Sunday, I was reentering the world of the living and really enjoyed a few days free of side effects.

Then yesterday, 3C (chemo kills cancer) day again. As I anticipated, my white cell and neutrophil counts were way too low to get my Fulfirinox. That means we can't go home Saturday. However, I did receive my gene therapy infusions yesterday and rescheduled my chemo to Friday and Monday.

We hope all will go well and we'll be on the road to Austin by Monday afternoon.

This is the first Thanksgiving in 40+ years I will not host turkey day. Jeff and Lisa are having the whole family out to their ranch, and I'm grateful we only need to bring a few simple dishes. I can't wait to be with all my kids and grandkids. Every family gathering becomes more precious.

I'm also realizing more each day what effect my continued struggles have on the grandkids.

Two weekends ago, Scott brought Carson (4) and Amelia (2) to spend the weekend with us. At that time, I had my external chemo pump attached to my port. Carson and Amelia were fascinated to learn all about the machine and tube going into my chest.

While Carson was touching the connectors, he looked up at me and said, "Nana, are you going to die?"

I immediately squeezed him. "No, sweetheart, that's why I'm taking this medicine and doing everything I can to get better."

While we're home, I rarely wear my wigs, so the grandchildren are comfortable seeing their bald Nana. That Sunday afternoon, I put on my wig to go to town.

As we were getting ready to leave, Amelia came into the kitchen, looked up at me, her eyes opened wide, her mouth dropped, and she said, "Nana, your hair came back!"

Out of the mouths of babes...

Thanksgiving, one of my favorite holidays, is only a week away. I wish all of you an abundant, loving, and restful Thanksgiving.

With love and gratitude,
K

"Bringing yourself to the Thanksgiving feast should be enough! :-)
Your mere presence is a testimony to your strength and fortitude.
You are giving kiddos right answers - they do better with the truth,
in simple terms. Then they won't be afraid.
I'm sorry this round is so difficult. You are in good hands in AR.
But you are Karen Strong!
When I count my blessings this Thanksgiving,
I will count you twice!! XO"
Kathy R

"Some days are harder than others in this journey.
Stay strong and faithful,
trust God to walk with you every step.
Keeping you in my prayers."
Cindy W

THE BEST CHRISTMAS PRESENT!
shrinking tumors for christmas

"Mrs. AMAZING Owen…
you are simply a remarkable badass and
I love you to pieces. Xoxo"
Rachel K

December 4, 2019

I didn't even notice the world for the last ten days. I have just survived a week of the worst chemo side effects since I was diagnosed almost two years ago, probably because I'm doing the simultaneous duo chemos.

I felt terrible a week ago Tuesday, our first day back in Austin. Then by Thanksgiving post-dinner, I scurried home to my beautiful designer bathroom for four days and only emerged this past Monday. I had even set up my tech tools—from cell phone to computer to remotes in my throne room—it was all at my fingertips.

It is just a great benefit that I have such a luxurious bathroom, but even that gets old…

The good news is that I went to my Austin oncologist yesterday. He gave me meds and a shot, and then sent me for an emergency CT scan to eliminate the possibility of a chemo-related infection. The scan results were good, so I have high hopes that cough medicine will conquer this lingering cough.

And as an added benefit of this interim CT, my Austin oncologist said my tumors have shrunk significantly since July.

Hallelujah and praise the Lord! What an unexpected gift on this beautiful day.

At this very moment, I am in the lobby of a surgical center waiting while Howard has his cataract surgery. Because Howard has vision in only one eye, we have felt anxious about the risk of this surgery. But since I have banned Howard from driving at night because of his poor vision, he decided the risk of surgery was better than listening to my daily harangues.

We'll be returning to AR next Tuesday so I can get my double dose chemo yet again, starting next Wednesday. Then, as soon as I feel up to the 18-hour drive (neither of us can fly), we'll cross the Great Plains and climb, climb, climb to our beloved Camp Owen Colorado for Christmas.

And the best news yet: ALL the kids and grandkids are joining us for the entire week of Christmas. All twenty of us will be together.

Hmmm... ten grandkids together in one house for a week? Thought Provoking...

Since I have been so sick for half of this Thanksgiving time at home, I haven't been able to see many of you Austinites who are so important to me. That doesn't mean I love or miss you any less. It just means we'll have to plan ahead for my next time in Austin starting Jan. 13.

In the interim, enjoy every minute getting ready for the holidays. Since none of us knows what God's plan is for us, savor every day and make each day count.

I do hope to see many of you over the next four days as we try to attend as many parties as possible. Now that I'm feeling better, I can't wait!

> With love, joy, and gratitude,
> Karen

"Wow 10 grand kids at Christmas!!
I can hardly handle 4. :) "
Mark K

"You continue to be an incredible inspiration to me.
My prayers are always with you!
I am amazed at what you accomplish and I know
God has His healing arms wrapped tightly around you.
May your Colorado Christmas be filled with
very special love and abundant MIRACLES!
Thank you for sharing your love, your hope, and your Christian spirit!
Love, hugs and prayers!"
Belinda K

CHRISTMAS LETTER
the Owen family

"I wish you and Howard a truly blessed Christmas
and a Healthy Happy New Year!
Enjoy your family at Camp Owen Colorado and
soak in the majesty of God's creation.
Sending Love and Peace your way."
Cindy W

December 17, 2019

Merry Christmas one and all!

Howard and I drove to CO Saturday and Sunday after I finished my most recent chemo treatments last Friday. The goal was to get up here before my side effects really kicked in this week - and the plan has worked.

We're enjoying the beauty and majesty of God's magnificent creation at the top of the mountains at our beloved Camp Owen Colorado. And other than being totally exhausted, I'm weathering the side effects pretty well this week - to the point where I'm putting up Christmas decorations before the kids and grandkids start arriving on Sunday.

Everyone is coming, so we'll have twenty immediate family members in the house over Christmas week.. I can't wait!

Howard is wary and remembers only too well how chaotic it was last year. But we can all survive one week, right?

Be sure to read my Christmas letter that follows. It comes with love and gratitude for all the support and prayers you have sent my way in 2019. Remember, I'm counting on you in 2020, too.

Have a blessed Christmas/holiday and be sure to keep in touch in the new year.

With love, joy, and gratitude,
Karen

"How wonderful to have all your family with you
for Christmas in the mountains!
Enjoy the time, and we look forward to hearing
about more great adventures with your family in 2020.
You are a true inspiration."
Nancy McC

Glory to God in the Highest and Peace and Goodwill to Man

On January 27, 2020, I will have battled Stage 4 Pancreatic/Liver cancer for 2 years. And though my 'new' life is severely restricted (Howard says that is compared to my 100 MPH normal pace) and ruled by doctors, chemo, radiation, shots, meds, supplements, +++. I AM STILL GOING STRONG. I know that you have followed my journey on Caring Bridge (caringbridge.org, karenowen2) because you have provided so much love and support throughout the last 2 years. It certainly has been a fast and furious time for our entire extended family – new homes, successful businesses, quickly growing grandchildren. We also honored the 6th anniversary of Averie's passing and the 2nd anniversary of losing our beloved Blake – still so much grief and so many tears. But as we close 2019, I am so grateful our entire family came together for Thanksgiving (see photos) and that all 20 of us will celebrate Christmas together at Camp Owen Colorado. More good news is that CO already has serious snow and visions of skiing, not sugarplums, dance in the grandkids' heads…

Howard has certainly kept busy this year; we have just celebrated our first year of Sapphire Homes in Northwest AR (www.sapphirehomesnwa.com) in partnership with our son Scott and daughter-in-law Liz – and already have a contract for one of our homes! Howard loves this new business and has become fully 'in' to building a production homebuilding company in NWA. Anyone who knows Howard knows he MUST have his comfortable, familiar 'space' (the architect in him shines through); we are now the proud owners of a comfy **Lake Cottage** on Beaver Lake in Eureka Springs. Once we decided to spend so much time in AR (I'm now doing all

chemo there), I remodeled our Lake Cottage (hidden in the jungles of Beaver Lake) at warp speed to draw family and friends to visit us. We have enough beds for our kids, spouses and 10 thriving grandkids (ages 1,2,2,5,5,7,10,10,12,14) whom we entice with our boat and ATVs. It is beautiful and peaceful at Lake Cottage – and a great place to meditate, rest, regroup and spend time with family and friends. It's also only a 9-hour drive from Austin, rather than the 19 hours to Camp Owen Colorado.

I am very grateful to be able to share these holidays with everyone important in my life. I believe it is God's will that I am still "movin'n'shakin". With His love, grace and support, I will continue to live each day to its fullest and enjoy the majesty and beauty of His creations both in the AR Ozarks and the Colorado Mountains.

Wishing you the Best of Everything in 2020!

With love, joy and gratitude,

Karen and Howard

LISA, JEFFREY FORD, RILEY, LANEY

STEVEN, LIAM, WESTYN, BRAZOS, SHANNON

LIZ, AMELIA, SCOTT, CARSON

KYLE, TIFFANY, KALEN, ETHAN

2020

HO HO HOS
SEEM SO LONG AGO!
a new year, a new decade

"This is such great news,
and I am so happy for you and your entire family,
who continue to fight
this damn disease with you."
Gigi R

January 12, 2020

I'm so glad it is a new year, a new decade... yet for some reason I'm striving to identify, I haven't felt like writing...

We had a magical Christmas with all the kids and grandkids: fresh crystalline snow, great skiing, sledding, snowman-making, evenings playing games, watching movies, laughing, telling stories. The only glitch was poor little Carson got altitude sickness for four miserable days and didn't get to ski, but he recovered and was soon happy playing outside in the snow with his cousins.

These are the memories I will carry in my heart forever.

I also won't soon forget that Howard and I drove to CO directly from AR since neither of us could fly (H recovering from cataract surgery and K having low immunity from chemo). So off we drove and soon accumulated $425 worth of speeding tickets, which convinced me we should only fly in the future!

I also figured out how to balance my grandmotherly duties with my energy levels. I always watch the little ones while our kids take their 5+-year-olds skiing. This year, with Carson feeling sick, he, Amelia, Brazos, and Ford stayed back at the house. On Nana days, I brought in a nanny and had some meals catered.

How did I get so smart? I was able to recuperate from chemo and be with my 'babies' at the same time.

Note to self: Do it again next year.

We left CO on December 30 for my dual chemo treatments in AR on January 2-4. I've been in a 'funk' for the last few weeks, so I decided it was time for me to come home to Austin to get re-grounded. I planned to leave AR as soon as I finished chemo so I wouldn't be on the road when the side effects hit again.

Howard needed to stay in AR, so I drove back last Sun/Mon (stayed overnight in Ft. Worth with my dear friend, Kathy), and arrived Monday in time for my therapy appt.

This week at home by myself has been timely, enlightening, and challenging. Time to regroup, prepare, and reflect. My therapist is delighted that I have progressed in my grief to anger. Yes, I am angry - cancer, Averie's loss, Blake's suicide, continued side effects, unknown chemo results... I'm using my solitude to work through these emotions and hope to get back to peace, love, gratitude - and to living each day to its max; not sinking into the past or trying to second-guess the future. Get back to taking it one day at a time.

Reset, reset, reset.

H is flying in Wednesday night, seeing his eye doctor on Thursday, and then we are heading back to AR Saturday. CT scan on January 20 and results on January 22. Will my tumors have shrunk? Is the new chemo working? Future treatments? Prognosis?

So much riding on this next CT. Please keep the prayers coming while I try to get my head back to where it needs to be.

I'm seeing my shaman Thursday and I know how good she is for me. I'm hoping to feel good enough to get out and around this week, soak in the energy and support of dear friends, and be ready for the return to AR and Howard's total focus on the new business.

I also hope sharing my angst resonates because knowing I can have a positive impact others is a boon to me. Know that I love and care... and on January 22 I will have great results to report.

With love and gratitude,
Karen

"Yes to a new year and new decade!
So glad Christmas in the mountains was great with your family!!
Laughing about your speeding tickets! ...
I hope this week is good for you.
You continue to have such strength and to see all the daily positives .
Sending you lots of love, and prayers for a good scan report."
Carol C

"HAPPY NEW YEAR!!
It was always great to hear all your wonderful stories
with family and Howard.
But more importantly your honesty in dealing
with everything and how you feel.
I so admire that... get it out!!
We are all here for you always...
Enjoy your time in Austin and safe travels back to AR.
No speeding!! ha ha... take care and
praying for good CT results in late January, much love."
Kendyl

A GREAT DAY!
5 rating

"The bumps in the road and constantly being tested in so many different ways.
We're sending loads of positive thoughts, laughter
(just look at the coat of arms Carl sent),
prayers, hugs, and love.
You have already earned Karen SPARKY Strong
a kizillion times over, as you're an amazing lady."
Lynn T

January 22, 2020

We've been back in AR since Saturday and awoke this morning to a beautiful light dusting of snow - coupled with a 20° wind chill. Shivering, we left at 7:30 AM to ensure plenty of time to see Dr. Beck for the long-anticipated results of Monday's CT scan. Then we were stopped dead-still on the road to town for a full hour while the police cleared an accident.

Tick-tock, tick-tock, ever so slowly goes the clock when you're waiting for important news.

At 9:30, Dr. Beck delivered the best news ever. My pancreatic tumor is stable and my liver tumors have shrunk 40% in the last 90 days since I've been getting the double chemo regimens of Fulferinox for the pancreatic cancer and Herceptin/Perjeta for my gene mutation. I asked Dr. Beck how he would rate me between 1 and 5, and without hesitation he said "5."

Praise the Lord! I just know He has heard all your prayers and I have experienced your love and unyielding support. I am just so excited and grateful.

What is next?

We are stopping the Fulfirinox for the time being. Again, thank the Lord! That Fulfirinox isn't known as the monster of all drugs for nothing, and I had the worst of all the bad side effects. So today I had the first of the single Perjeta/Herceptin infusions; now the plan is to take these treatments every three weeks with a follow-up CT scan in nine weeks. We're trying to see if the Perjeta/Herceptin stops my positive HER2 mutation, the cause of continued tumor growth. So stop, stop, stop the tumors with this treatment and my future should look good - at least for the next eight months on this regimen.

I also saw my Shaman last Friday. So glad I did. My core is more stable and stronger than in previous visits. She also suggested some new approaches in dealing with my complex grief. Let me try some of her suggestions and I'll write about results in the near future.

But one thing she said has 'stuck' with me over the past week: "Say YES to life!" Instead of fearing what else may happen in my life, I need to change my entire approach to fear and grief and jump back in to all that I may face and "Say YES to life!"

That is just what I intend to do. Taking it one day at a time...

> With love and gratitude,
> Karen Sparky Strong

P.S. Yep, I'm still taking my PanacurC, meditating, therapy, my shaman, prayer, focusing on my friends, reading, +++ - yet I need to step up on my restricted diet and exercise.

> "Best news!
> Keep kicking ass, my friend!
> Love and Hugs!!"
> Rachel K

> "Knowing me, I'm never lost for words!
> But I can't even put into words how I feel
> about your good news and hope!
> I am definitely doing my happy dance today."
> Bonnie F

Celebrate! Celebrate!
Dance to the Music!
potassium is so important

"HAPPY AMAZING ANNIVERSARY!"
Mark K

January 28, 2020

TWO YEARS! Two whole years since my original diagnosis.

I couldn't imagine I would be overlooking Beaver Lake Arkansas from our Lake Cottage two years after the doctors gave me as little as three weeks to live with an advanced diagnosis of Stage 4 pancreatic and liver cancer on January 27, 2018. In fact, I had no inkling I would be basking in this remote isolation and soaking in the crystal-clear water of this gorgeous oasis.

But by the grace of God, here I am!

The journey to AR began 3½ years ago when Scott moved to Fayetteville for a job promotion… and the rest is history. Howard and I decided to partner with Scott and Liz in a production building company and here we are -

Howard has always wanted to do this and wishes he had started this business 20 years ago; I'm just glad he has a focus and purpose.

Fifteen months into Sapphire Homes, we have a viable business that Howard loves and a beautiful lake cottage (that makes Howard feel like he is semi-retired while really being a workaholic). And I have found a top-notch oncologist (in AR) who has managed to treat me with a very expensive drug for FREE that we hope will stop my gene mutation and control my tumor growth. We'll know in eight weeks.

In the interim, I am fighting the good fight daily; yesterday and today I am getting potassium infusions to raise my pitifully low levels. I have learned so much on this journey. For example, did you know that low and high levels of potassium can cause cardiac arythmia? I'm amazed at the great care I am receiving at the Highlands Oncology Group in Bentonville, AR. In fact, Howard and I both believe my care here is better than at either MD Anderson or Austin.

The medical learning journey is just one small piece of the winding path of the last two years. More importantly, my spiritual journey has redefined me. I realize I am not in control. The Lord has a plan for me and my role is to be the best I can be in alignment with faith, hope, and love. Let go of the past (trying to eliminate guilt and regrets), don't try to control the future (it is God's plan, not mine), and live each day one day at a time.

I think this devotional is very insightful: "A life worth living has these ingredients. It has a creed - what we believe. It has a code - how we behave. And it has a character - what we become."

Every day with cancer brings new struggles; cancer rules my life. I seem defined by each day's challenges. But as long as God gives me the physical and mental strength, I will persevere. In fact, with God's support, I will be writing another journal one year from today - on my third anniversary of survival.

Keep praying, supporting, loving me as we search for healing and a cure. Isn't it appropriate that this is today's Bible verse? "Don't worry, because I am with you. Don't be afraid, because I am your God. I will make you strong and will help you; I will help you with my right hand that saves you." - Isaiah 41:10.

What a journey! What an amazing two years. What a personal transformation. Now looking forward to many more years of sharing my life, one day at time.

> With so much love and gratitude,
> Karen Sparky Strong

> "You are an inspiration!
> We have an awesome God who performs great miracles,
> and creates the beauty in the world around us.
> Your verse for today says it all - hold on to His right hand,
> and you WILL be writing another journal entry this day next year.
> May His Peace be with you,
> and continue to carry you to complete health."
> Leah L

MORE TESTS OF FAITH
Lauren's 2nd big unexpected loss

"My sign-off on my emails, actually on life is,
'Life is a gift, live each day with gratitude and hope for the future.'
You, my dear, personify that.
Keep the faith, dear Karen, and persevere.
With love from your 'Chicago' cousins..."
Gigi and Joe

February 4, 2020

With each passing day, we miss Blake more, we continuously talk to him - and I ask him constantly for his support and help to conquer my cancer. Most of all, he is always by our side.

Last week, I received a call from Lauren's (Blake's wife) mom, informing us that the young man Lauren had been dating for the last 15 months had died during the night. He was a very fit and healthy 38-year-old man who loved Lauren enough to allow her to celebrate Blake and Lauren's anniversary, Blake's birthday, +++ or just to talk about him.

Needless to say, Sabin's sudden heart attack and death evoked shock, deep emotions, and our greatest sadness and sympathy for Lauren. It has only been 2½ years since we lost Blake, and now she has lost Sabin, the first man she has dated since Blake.

How could the Lord put her through this? I have lost sleep, have cried for her - and for Blake... and am truly troubled for Lauren and how she will be able to absorb this new and significant loss. This new event has ripped the healing band-aid off the wound of Blake's death all over again.

Then this morning, Lauren's mom sent me the eulogy she gave at Sabin's funeral yesterday. Her words stopped me right in my tracks - and it is so relevant to surviving death, cancer, or ???

Liz Tuttle said:

"I don't understand God's plan for taking Sabin from us at 38 and I don't like it. I don't like the way it looks and feels this side of heaven...

"But the Word of God reminds me that His ways and his thoughts are higher than mine, that He is for us and not against us, that we are just foreigners on this earth, passing through to our true and eternal home in heaven. Jesus promises us he will not leave us or forsake us and when we weep, he weeps. He will walk through this valley of the shadow of death with us; when we are faint of heart, He will be our covering and our strong tower, and we can find refuge under his wing and when we are weak, He is strong! He is our hope, He is faithful, He is good, and He is trustworthy...

So we must cling to Him and we must trust. Sabin knew and trusted the God who created him and he knew nothing could separate him from the love of God, not even death for those who are in Christ Jesus."

In another part of her eulogy, Liz wrote:

"I once saw a demonstration a lady did with a piece of needlepoint. The back-side was full of stray threads and dark colors and knots and tangles. It wasn't pretty and didn't make sense... just like how life can be at times. It almost made you want to throw it away. But then she turned it over to display the most beautiful picture. That's a perfect example of our Heavenly Father saying... 'My dear children, keep the faith and go about my business here on earth, the place that's broken and sometimes doesn't make sense and then someday I will bring you to heaven and you will see the beautiful design from my perspective and you wouldn't change a thing.'"

What Liz wrote has helped remind me of my spiritual goals and commitment as I work through these long and challenging weeks of not responding to treatments to bring up my potassium and white/red blood cells and platelets. This walking around as a human germ magnet with low immunities and exhaustion is not the road I choose.

Liz's words hit me right between the eyes. Every day brings new challenges. OH - News Flash - I just received my blood results from today AND my potassium levels are finally UP. Praise the Lord - now I don't have to go to the doctor until my next chemo treatment on February 12.

Slow and steady as she goes - focus, focus, focus on continued healing! Happy Valentine's Day!

With love and gratitude,
Karen

"Thank you for sharing those beautiful words
from a grieving mother.
It really puts life (and death) into perspective.
I continue to be moved and inspired by your faith, your strength,
and your positive outlook.
Prayers for you and your battle with this dreadful disease."
Mari L

"I was so saddened to read this entry.
What a heartbreak for Lauren. Hope she stays strong.
Your posts are always so encouraging and hopeful,
even when you face sad news.
I often think about Blake, and am so glad to hear
that his memories offer you support."
Raghbir K

"ENOUGH ALREADY!!!!
What a beautiful eulogy given by a mom
who is so sad for her grieving daughter... again.
We are constantly taught from others through God's word.
Let that be a lesson to us today. Thank you so much for sharing.
Keeping you in my prayers, friend. XO"
Denise H

My Membership to The Ultimate Spa
an unusual euphemism

"Love your positivity!
No doubt you've developed special friendships at the spa
because that's who you are… always looking to help others.
Always in your court, Karen Strong!"
Pam W

February 5, 2020

I belong to a very select 'spa' that has an extremely high entry fee and greater monthly fees than most people could ever pay. Everyone there knows my name. As I nestle into a large comfy La-Z-Boy chair, a kind smiling lady brings me some filtered water (I'd prefer Prosecco) and a heated blanket. That sets the stage for great discussions with the other spa guests - and that's how new friendships begin.

In fact, my new friend Kathy and I are having lunch after our spa visit on February 12. As another new acquaintance said, "The membership here is so limited that you have to be identified by God as Special - and only then will your membership be considered."

Walking through the doors is very selective and 'wanting' is certainly not enough. I spend enough time there that I continue to learn, to support others, to find strength in others' stories. What a great new discovery and community center. I just had to rethink how these new spa members impact my life.

Yes, you guessed it. This 'spa' is my euphemism for the Oncology infusion lab here in NW AR, where I have found the kindest and most dedicated nurses, patients who spend so much of their lives in the oncology center (like me), and the humor to call my chemo treatments and lab work "spa treatments."

And yes, I'm probably losing it, but why not with a smile and tongue-in-cheek… Makes for a good story, and I'm sticking to it.

The next time I share my 'day at the spa', don't burst my bubble! I get a lot done there, from writing to reading to great discussions to learning about new treatments to... whatever! A far cry from IBM but still relevant to my current priorities.

> Pushing forward,
> Karen

"You never cease to find a great story to tell.
Keep 'em comin'! "
Jane B

"I love the concept of a spa where you can relax, reflect, and fantasize.
Richard and I have two new friends here at THE VILLAGE
who have bi-weekly infusions for Multiple Myeloma at Texas Oncology.
I will share your story with them.
We had snow last night... around 10:00 p.m. and this morning,
the Triangle Park area was white.
The dogs who were out for exercise seemed to tread lightly!!
Keep up the super spirit... one day at a time."
Martha C

"Your positive outlook makes us all feel good."
Love you."
Kathy C

Happy Valentine's Day
"The Oak Tree"
a message of encouragement

"Happy Valentine's Day to you, Karen!
Your heart, your love is endless.
I am with you in spirit! Xoxo"
Rosemary L

February 14, 2020

Happy Valentine's Day to the Love of My Life! (Yes, that would be HHO!)

On our 52nd Valentine's Day together since we met at the University of Illinois. Quite a life we have shared... and I plan to share for years to come. I'll love you forever, Howard!

My thoughts today are disparate: Numbers and Poetry. Really?

First the numbers - I haven't given you my tumor marker numbers since fall of 2019. Then Wednesday, while I was getting my gene mutation chemo, the P.A. was so excited about my latest CA19-9 and CEA results that she came running in to the lab to share results with me in person. Since my diagnosis 2 years ago, my numbers have been bad and better. For example, my CEA was once 3500; 3 months ago it was 177 and this week it is now 27, a remarkable improvement. My CA19-9 has been steady for the last 4 months when the # was 17 and is now 19, which is still considered excellent for anyone with my diagnosis.

Celebration and gratitude are in order.

The rest of my blood work still shows low red and white blood cells, platelets, adrenal function, immune function, liver function - and on and on and on. I have contracted with Nutritional Profiles out of Dallas whose owner,

Jim Judd, specializes in oncology patients. Based on my specific blood work and historical data from his comprehensive database of other patients, Jim is recommending a program of food and supplements designed just for me.

The goal will be to break up the dysfunctional elements by groups over the next 6-12 months, e.g., we're going to treat for Red Blood Cell Function, Adrenal Function, Immune Function, Liver Function, Gallbladder Function and GI Function first. Then we'll move on to the next critical group in areas such as Vitamins, Electrolytes, Protein Need, +++

I feel very hopeful in taking a specific, scientific approach to my blood balancing needs. Stay tuned.

I continue to be surprised and grateful for so many ongoing gifts and cards; I read, reread, and save every single one. This week, one of the beautiful cards I received contained a truly memorable poem which I want to share with you as we all need encouragement at one time or another...

"The Oak Tree" - A Message of Encouragement

A mighty wind blew night and day,
It stole the oak tree's leaves away,
Then snapped its boughs and pulled its bark
Until the oak was tired and stark.
But still the oak tree held its ground
While other trees fell all around.
The weary wind gave up and spoke,
"How can you still be standing, Oak?"
The oak tree said, "I know that you
Can break every branch of mine in two,
Carry every leaf away,
Shake my limbs and make me sway.
But I have roots stretched in the earth,
Growing stronger since my birth.
You'll never touch them, for you see
They are the deepest part of me.
Until today, I wasn't sure
Of just how much I could endure.
But now I've found, with thanks to you,
I'm stronger than I ever knew."

With love and gratitude,
Karen Sparky Strong

"Love the poem!
You are that Oak tree for sure.
Happy Valentine's Day!"
Cindy J

3 GREAT DAYS - AND COUNTING
da da da da da da = me singing

"You are such an inspiration to all of us.
So glad to hear your voice on the phone each week,
and to know God is leading you to some amazing doctors
in your healing process.
We are praying for you! Sending you love and hugs."
Leigh

February 27, 2020

The feel-good days have finally arrived! I am now in my fourth day of no digestive problems - and I feel good - da da da da da da da (*that is me singing*). Since I started on the supplements recommended by my nutritionist specialist in Dallas, I've experienced continuous improvement.

I'll find out next Wednesday (next chemo day) if my blood test results improve. In the interim, I'm lovin' feeling so good. Energy improving, no pain, minimal digestive issues – praise the Lord and all the prayers from YOU - my fantastic support group. Fingers crossed for more of the same.

With love and gratitude,
Karen Sparky Strong

"Happy dance!
You made me feel better today!
What supplements are you taking
that the doctor recommended?"
Bonnie F

Covid-19 (aka Coronavirus)
the pandemic of our lifetime

"If you open the dictionary and you see the word 'admiration'
there it is: your picture!
I truly admire you for how you are going through this,
no words can express!
You definitely are God's child!"
Bonnie F

March 15, 2020

All our lives have changed so quickly, with social media and global comms ensuring we know every day what's happening with Covid-19 in every nook and cranny of the globe. With social distancing, event cancellations, and even school closings, we're experiencing a new and uncomfortable normal. I sure don't like this any better than 'the next guy,' and I'm in the highest risk group, being a 70+ chemo patient.

I am self-quarantined in my jammies at our Lake Cottage, enjoying the beautiful view of Beaver Lake and sitting in front of the fire to ward off the damp chill of the NW AR wintery March. I am so grateful to be in this life stage where I have time to focus on recovery from my primary challenge: cancer. I am so aware of suffering of millions and am praying for those whose lives are in total devastation and chaos.

And of course, I'm asking WHY all the tornadoes, hurricanes, forest fires, and now Covid-19? Is the Lord trying to 'tell' us something? If nothing else, this pandemic should bring all peoples together united against a common enemy. This gives new meaning to "Live each day and don't sweat the small stuff."

The last time I wrote, I was feeling sooo good. Then a week ago Wednesday, I had chemo which brought the ensuing week of bad side effects - total exhaustion, digestive challenges, depression, and self-sought isolation. A week ago, I also caught a cold, developed a sore throat and laryngitis.

I am so lucky to have Howard, my concerned adult children, and my steadfast friends checking on me as I navigate this repeating cycle. And guess what? I'm now on the cyclical upswing - regaining some energy and not spending all day in the bathroom.

Hallelujah! Praise the Lord! And thank you for all your ongoing prayers.

Kyle, Tiffany, Ethan, and Kalen were supposed to be coming to visit us in AR this week. Now they are not coming, unless I call and give them an 'all clear.' What should I do?

Since the CO house is empty, Austin schools are closed, and Steven's company is working remotely, the five of them are on their way to CO and don't even know when they'll return to Austin. How's that for a positive silver lining?

While we wrestle with long grocery lines, empty shelves, not seeing our loved ones, or not living our full life, I hope you will count the ways we are blessed. We all have to believe each one of us will survive and walk away with a new appreciation of health/life. I'm sure you're receiving the plethora of new articles, songs, and prayers related to the virus.

So many are suffering in ways that we can't imagine; the challenges seem so overwhelming to me. "Lord have mercy and grant us peace..."

Pushing through with love and gratitude,
Karen Sparky Strong

"Even when you are going through tough times,
your optimism and positive view of live shines through.
Now is a tough time for all of us with the uncertainty we all are facing.
I am emulating your perspective. Stay positive,
take one day at a time, and appreciate the love of friends and family.
Thank you for being such a good role model.
Stay hunkered down! Enjoy your beautiful view! .
And find a good book to read!"
Peggy H

"Yes, counting the ways we are blessed.
You have such a gift for saying what so many of us are feeling.
Take care of yourself!"
Kathy G

Isolated In The Hospital – Surgery All Alone
scared and stressed

"I'm praying silently, out loud, standing up, sitting down...
every way I can think of, dear one."
Marion M

March 25, 2020

And Howard can't even visit. But then, we're all sort-of in the same boat. Thank goodness for Facetime and Zoom, because the alternative would truly be total isolation.

Monday was the long-awaited day for my EEG and CT to determine the efficacy of the Herceptin/Perjeta drug trial I have been on for the last 3 months. If you recall, Dr. Beck had secured the drug for me free from Genentech for a Pancreatic patient "Trial of 1 (ME)." (The cost in Austin was $9500 per treatment because my insurance wouldn't cover).

Thank God for Dr. Beck. But the jury is still out on results, though Dr. Beck says my liver looks the same as it did three months ago, which is good news vs. my new news.

I was waiting for my results TODAY. When I saw my oncologist's # on my phone yesterday morning, my heart raced, my blood pressure rose, and with shaking hand I answered Dr. Beck's call. I knew he wasn't calling with good news, but I wasn't prepared for his message.

He wanted me to go directly to the hospital (I'm here now) to have a stent surgically implanted into a blocked bile duct. But the worst part of his news is that the bile duct is blocked by a cancerous lymph node. That means my cancer has spread to my lymph nodes.

So now what? We won't know until the surgery is successful and my dangerously high bilirubin count drops back to normal.

What's next? Right now, the whites of my eyes are scary yellow, and so is my skin. On Friday, Howard and I will sit down with Dr. Beck and look at options.

News flash: the nurse just told me I won't have the surgery until tomorrow morning. Ugh! So frustrating.

My CT results validated an outcome I hoped never to face, but here we are. New cancer and limited plans for future treatment because I have the dreaded no-cure pancreatic cancer. I just can't endure another round of Fulfirinox, cyber knife radiation won't work, and I have a phobia against traditional radiation.

Can't wait to see what Dr. Beck has up his sleeve. He has mentioned a possible new trial.

I will admit I am bummed, scared, stressed, and depressed. Scott and Liz are sick, Jeff was exposed to Covid-19 yesterday, Sapphire Homes and Kaemark are severely impacted by Covid-19, and so many Americans are suffering so much... Have to remember the mantra: One day at a time.

I hope and pray you are doing as well as possible during these turbulent days. I feel like the only thing we can do is pray.

Until Friday,
Karen

"Bless Your Heart, Karen!
My prayers are with you and your family.
You are STILL stronger than you think and
HE is in control, so do not be afraid!"
Mari L

"I'm praying for you daily.
You are an amazing woman,
and I know there be another plan.
Hang in there! xoxo"
Ree O

"Thinking of you SO much, Karen,
and sending up lots of prayers.
Hang in there, my strong warrior!!!! XOXO"
Denise H

If Interested: All About Tomorrow's Surgery
medical lesson #?

"Yes, one day at a time –
and maybe throw in a few of
your infectious laughs for good measure!
(I'm sure you are)
Much love, hugs, and prayers!"
Sara VS

March 25, 2020

Hi again,

I've never written two entries in one day, but since I'm just lounging in bed in the hospital, I thought some inquiring minds might be interested in the surgery I'm having in the morning. Read on, if the bug bites.

My surgery is at 9 in the morning. I'm very impressed with the gastroenterologist, Dr. O'Keefe, who shared that he is bringing in a more senior experienced surgeon to observe and help if necessary. The surgery is complicated because of my cancer. I will be under general anesthetic, intubated, and then a scope through my mouth to the stomach and into the intestines, liver and/or pancreas. The doctor will insert a plastic tube into the bile duct, which will need to be replaced every two months until the current situation changes.

If the cancerous lymph nodes get worse, the doctor will insert a permanent steel stent. If enlarged node shrinks, they will stop replacing the plastic stents.

This is truly a next level of the disease's progress and one I didn't want to get to. I hope to go home Friday and be able to meet with Dr. Beck to agree on a new plan to attack the cancerous lymph nodes. Desired surgery outcomes: reduced diarrhea, lowered bilirubin count (so I won't be yellow), and let digestives enzymes flow through to the small intestines. Hoping for the optimal results.

I also have a very infected finger, so the 'wound team' came in and gave me an ointment and put me on Keflex. Who would have thought such a little thing would become so important? But all infections are threatening in these times.

There you have it. And you're one step closer to your medical degree! (-:

Until Friday,
Karen

"You have never stopped teaching me a thing or two!
Sending positive energy right to you!"
Jane B

"You and your family are always in our hearts and prayers.
Big hugs as you continue your journey as Karen STRONG!!!
We are with you 100% of the way as we read your updates…
keep them coming. We are on this journey with you!!!"
Susie D

"Sending prayers for optimal results tomorrow.
Your doctors sound amazing,
and I know you are in great hands.
I ask God for protection tomorrow as you undergo surgery."
Suzanne M

Ever Slept Through The Night in a Hospital?
freezing out a fever, stenting a bile duct

"We are praying for you, Karen.
May God grant you, and all of us, a path to good health.
Stay strong! We are thinking of you and
sending positive thoughts daily."
Gigi R

March 27, 2020

Can't imagine answering yes.

As you know, yesterday was my big surgery day and I now have a permanent metal stent to open that bile duct and push the cancerous lymph node back. The doctors said all went well yesterday, saw lots of drainage, but as of now, my bilirubin count is NOT dropping and my liver enzymes are not improving.

Total bummer. More tests at noon, and then we'll know if I can go home tonight. Fingers and toes crossed - but not very optimistic.

It really scared me last night when I started running fever. It is foreboding where the mind immediately jumps. I can't take Advil, aspirin, Tylenol, or anything that processes through the liver - especially not now! So the nurses removed my blankets and turned the AC way down. *Voila!* That fever was so cold it ran out the door in search of some other unsuspecting victim. (-:

I'm watching the *Today Show* and see that the number of Covid-19 cases in the US have surpassed every other nation. Yesterday, I received a global prayer chain request (growing to more than 2M people) to say the Lord's Prayer and then to pass this request to at least eight other people.

Dear Lord, please hear our prayers...

I expected to be in the hospital for one night, and now I'm going on four. I wasn't prepared for an extended stay, so I'm now wearing those humbling hospital gowns, stretched out socks, and no make-up. That's no make-up to cover my yellow skin - and then there's my yellow eyeballs. Argh! And NO visitors.

If I'm here much longer, Howard may even expand his skill set to include running the dishwasher, washer, and/or dryer. (I won't hold my breath.)

I'm falling asleep after my sleepless night. SAY SAFE AND HEALTHY! Zzzzzz

Trying to be Karen Sparky Strong!
Keep those prayers coming...

"Sending my superwoman strength, my super batwoman powers*,
and my super feisty batmobile to ZOOM you back home
to heal and recover on Friday !!
The sun shining always targets a natural smile.
Looking forward to those smiles. Xoxo
* piles of fist bumps until the virus looms to a distant nowhere."
Courtney R

"If the doctors get overwhelmed,
they could always have you speak to their patients
and explain everything because you are well trained!
Keep on keeping on! Praying for you every day will get better."
Bonnie F

"You are an amazing inspiration to me and so many others.
Our God is an amazing healer.
My prayers are for total healing for you, sweet friend.
May God give you strength and hope, and rid your body of this horrific cancer.
You have such an unselfish heart! Get rest and keep that positive spirit.
I know there are visitors in the room with you, if only in spirit!
God is by your side always! Big hugs and big prayers!"
Belinda K

TRIAL FAILED
home in my big jacuzzi tub full of bubbles

"I was sitting on my back deck thinking about you on your back deck.
I am so glad you have returned home and Howard is at your side.
You are oh, so strong, Karen Strong Owen.
Hugs, kisses, and may you feel God's ever-present comfort."
Auddie W

March 28, 2020

It is so great to be home. I leisurely bathed in my big jacuzzi tub full of bubbles, then slid between my silky heavenly-blue sheets while I lay my head on my familiar old pillow Howard named 'Two-Feathers' because it is so flat. Then I sank into a deep sleep wrought by exhaustion from my hospital stay. I had gone in Tuesday afternoon, thinking I'd be home by Wednesday night, yet ended up staying until Saturday.

I have such empathy and have prayed for those Covid-19 patients who cannot have visitors in the hospital and in many cases die alone. I understand that feeling of isolation, since even Howard couldn't visit me.

I won't soon forget receiving the news Tuesday that my cancer had spread to my lymph node—alone. I was prescribed an antibiotic for my infected finger and then got the news that I also have a bladder infection—alone. I won't ever forget the fear and anxiety of prepping for surgery and then waking up—alone.

I was alone when they told me yesterday I couldn't go home because my bilirubin was not decreasing and I might have to undergo another procedure (which I am thankful didn't happen.) And then today I learned—alone—that the current trial with Herpicin/Perjeta has failed for me. I not only have cancer in my lymph node, but I also have four cancerous nodes in my lungs and some of my old tumors have grown again.

Needless to say, I was exuberant to see Howard waiting for me at the main entrance of the hospital after my devastating news today.

During my entire hospital stay, an indigent woman four doors down had a total psychological breakdown and has been there for a month, and all she does throughout the day and night is scream "Help, please help me, +++" Listening to that was quite disturbing and like nails on the chalkboard; I just couldn't take it any more and insisted on changing rooms. That's probably one reason they sent me home today. So why is she still there? Sadly, they can't find anywhere else for her to go.

This was a pretty tough week and I'm trying to digest it all. My oncologist, Dr. Beck, has now enrolled me in another trial, which is supposed to start in three weeks, although there has already been one delay because of Covid-19. I'm keeping my fingers crossed that the trial begins as planned because I am his #1 pancreatic cancer patient in the trial. This trial is a combination of drugs (not chemo) and immunotherapy. There are 20 institutions across the country participat ing in this trial: MD Anderson in Houston is one of them and Highlands Oncology Group here in NW AR is another.

I had plenty of time to think and pray during my hospital stay. I can't say I've figured anything out yet, but what I learned today is certainly sobering and scary. I think I need to plop myself on our deck overlooking the beautiful and tranquil lake and process all of this. I need to work my way through this 'funk.'

From Isaiah:

> Fear not, for I am with you;
> be not dismayed for I am your God;
> I will strengthen you,
> I will help you,
> I will uphold you with my righteous right hand.

So many of you are reaching out to me multiple times a day. I'm sorry I just don't have the time or stamina to respond to each of you. But know that I cherish every call and message, and that your support, love and prayers mean everything to me. I'm going to need even more support and love in upcoming weeks and months.

Without a doubt, the best outcome would be success in this next trial... Lord, please hear our prayers...

With love, gratitude and trepidation,
Karen

"Dear Lord, we ask of you success in the next trial Karen Strong will endure,
Lord, hear our prayers... Amen."
Gigi R

Happy Monday Morning
what do you know about Bilirubin?

"Having setbacks must be terribly hard,
more than I could comprehend.
Please continue to be so positive in your fight.
You are not called 'Sparky Strong' for nothing!
What happy news about grandchild #12!"
Nancy McC

April 6, 2020

I'm so grateful to begin a new week. You already know about my hospital stay a week ago. Again I thought the worst was behind me. A week ago Monday started pretty normal; I had to go to the doctor. Monday and Tuesday to closely track my blood and bilirubin.

Thank the Lord, my bilirubin has been dropping, albeit quite slowly. But that is okay; I'll take slow progress any day.

Then the sky fell in again. I woke Wednesday morning with a sore neck as if I had slept wrong. By Thursday, my entire neck was frozen and stiff, and by Thursday night, I was in excruciating pain with shooting/throbbing lightning bolts throughout all the blood vessels in my brain.

I knew what it was because I had the same thing 23 years ago, and I'll never forget the pain or the following six long months on steroids. Anyway, after tests and another CT, I was diagnosed with Cerebral Vasculitis (swelling of the blood vessels in the brain). The doctor immediately put me on a megadose of prednisone, pain killers, prescription stomach-lining meds, and anti-anxiety med. Yes, this is caused by stress.

By Saturday, I improved significantly and today only my neck is still stiff and sore. I went to the doctor today and will go again Wednesday to monitor the swelling and my bilirubin/blood. I am so blessed to have such a caring and responsive medical team.

My bilirubin was 4.1 this morning, which is still too high to resume chemo or get into the trial. The next three weeks will be critical for my bilirubin to drop below 2 . So that's my next medical goal and, I hope, God's plan for me.

On a happy note: Shannon and Steven are having their fourth baby, a little girl who will be born in October. We are so excited. This will bring our grandchild count to one dozen.

Grandparenting is the best role in the world! And God willing, Covid-19 will be behind us and I will be in good shape. I am a baby-mama and can't

 wait to cuddle, kiss, and babysit for my last but not least grandchild.

Stay safe!!!

With love and gratitude,
Karen Sparky Strong

"Are grand kids cheaper by the dozen? :)"
Mark K

"Your letters to the home front resemble the Book of Job.
So pleased to hear about a new baby in the family.
New life gives us hope.
We look forward to seeing a happy picture of you
holding the latest grandchild.
And to the day you are free from those nasty cells.
Much affection to you and Howard."
Mary C

As Dolly Would Say, "Here You Come Again..."
quarantining in AR

April 16, 2020

Here's hoping the third time is a charm.

The trial I was hoping for already failed, so not an option for me. The dosages were too toxic and 50% of the small test group continued to have tumor growth after a month in the trial. So Dr. Beck put me back on chemo yesterday (bad day of side effects but better today).

But I didn't want to go back on that monster Fulfirinox for a third time, so we agreed on a new chemo cocktail called Gemzar/Abraxane. (Remember, I'm helping you keep your mind sharp. There will soon be a quiz to assess your memory and mental acuity.) Well, the difference is that the side effects should be less intense, but the data show that the results are also less effective.

We're off into the unknown again and I will have my next CT can on May 27 to assess the effectiveness of this new approach. One of the drawbacks is that I have the chemo infusions three weeks on and one week off.

In addition to sheltering in place in AR because of Covid-19, I'm also locked in up here for chemo treatments. We have not been home to Austin since December, and I am missing my TX kids and grandkids so much, my heart actually hurts. But we haven't seen Scott, Liz, Carson, or Amelia up here either because of Covid-19. I'm hoping that will soon change.

Liz had Covid for six weeks in February/March and just got her test back that she is now Negative. So grateful she is already feeling better; it was a long difficult six-weeks, and because she didn't have the 'typical' symptoms, none of us even knew she had Covid. In fact, I was with her a lot in February, so it is rather miraculous that I didn't get it from her.

The Lord sure works in mysterious ways: while my tumors were growing, I didn't contract Covid.

With Scott, Liz, and me all sick, Howard has been holding down the business front all by himself. He will be the first to admit he is exhausted. Praise the Lord! Scott and Liz are now better and getting back into the world of our fledgling homebuilding company.

When Howard came home today, he said, "I'm firing myself tomorrow at 5:00 from the superintendent's part of my job. Starting Monday, all this construction @#% is back in Scott's control."

Howard has learned so much as acting superintendent and has gained a new respect and appreciation for Scott, a good thing all around. Now we just need homebuyers!

I must admit, since my isolated hospital stay few weeks ago, I have been unable to forget all those sick people who are dying alone in isolation. I've also been sorely impacted by the number of deaths our first responders face on a daily basis. I am now working to reduce my stress and anxiety levels to overcome the trauma I am feeling; I sure do wish my left eye would stop twitching.

That said, I am SO GRATEFUL for the beauty and serenity of our lake cottage in the hinterland of Beaver Lake. Our family is all healthy and ensconced in their homes and with food on the table. To mentally survive this, I also have faith that God does have a plan for our global recovery.

Stay safe!
Karen Sparky Strong

"Karen Sparky Strong, you continue to inspire and amaze!
Your positive attitude will guide you through the day to day.
Remember to stay in the moment and present
and take things day by day.
Third time is a charm for sure!
Grateful your family is returning to good health and staying safe,
and that Howard will semi-fire himself today at 5 ;).
How awesome you can enjoy your beautiful surroundings.
It sounds very comforting and peaceful!
Sending positive thoughts and hugs!"
Pam W

I CHOOSE
THE JOY OF LIVING!
life in the time of covid

"I love reading your thought-provoking, hope-filled, positive messages
and the sharing of your very personal cancer journey.
You're so eloquent, fun, uplifting, and your words are much appreciated
always. I too wonder how life will change (or not), after Covid-19.
I'm hopeful for a slower, more appreciative life and lifestyle, which I can control.
More global awareness, that we are all in this together
on our small planet. And... welcoming my first grandchild.
Love to you and your family, Karen! Prayers for you all!"
Sharon W

April 24, 2020

Oh no, oh no, oh no.

I just posted today's journal (I think it was pretty good) and it is GONE, deleted, not there. I must have accidentally hit a wrong button because my wonderful words of wisdom are nowhere to be found...

Sigh. Do you know that sinking feeling? What do I do now?

Well, I don't have time to rewrite, so I'm going to just summarize the bullet points... here goes.

Want to share with you:

Make sure you test positive for Faith.
Keep your distance from Doubt, and isolate yourself from Fear.
Trust in God through it all. - Kelly's Treehouse +++.

I had my first new chemo treatment ten days ago. Despite a promise of lesser side effects, that DID NOT happen. So sick for eight days. And when I went back last Wednesday for infusion #2, the PA informed me my platelets were sooo low, I couldn't get my treatment. They sent me home to eat lots of protein, get plenty of sleep, and then we'll reassess next Wed.

Good thing I love our bedroom at Owen Lake Cottage because I sure am spending an exorbitant amount of time under the covers.

Still anxious about Covid, and actually having the test this afternoon because I was with Liz so much when she had it and we didn't know she had it. Stay tuned.

Please pray for God's grace in the passing of Gene Feller, a friend who was diagnosed with pancreatic cancer one year ago and has been with end-of-life Hospice care in Austin. Rest in peace, Gene.

I am committed to the JOY of Living, and yesterday was one of those days. It was our grandson Ethan's 15th birthday and our granddaughter Riley's 11th birthday. We all joined a Google Meet for a virtual dinner, sang 'Happy Birthday,' and drooled as Tiffany served triple-chocolate cake to Ethan. Talk about envy! Ethan and Riley will always remember their 2020 birthdays - and so will we.

I have a task for you. Would you please send me your thoughts on what our new normal will look like? What things will never come back? What new things will we do? How can we sustain our cleaner environment?

I can't wait to hear what you think…

Time to run. Have a great weekend.

> With love and gratitude,
> K Sparky Strong

"Your words are so true and you are such an inspiration.
I'm looking forward to seeing you again soon…
even if it is just across the driveway!!
One of my favorite verses is Romans 5:3-6:
'We rejoice in our suffering knowing
that suffering produces perseverance;
perseverance, character, and character, hope.
And hope does not disappoint us as God pours his love
into our hearts through the Holy Spirit which he has given us.'
Sending prayers and a hug!! Love you!."
Julie M

VHS
I am Vital, Healthy, Strong

"Enjoy your TGIF and seeing your kids! I love your VHS!
You continue to inspire, God is great! Praying for you always!"
Belinda K

April 30, 2020

If you are reading this, you are probably old enough to remember what is now old-timey technology known as a VHS tape. In fact, unless you've made the change to digital, all your irreplaceable family movies are probably still on those VHS tapes, and fading fast!

Today, I have associated new meaning for VHS. I do try to expand and change my daily affirmations with my morning meditations. Unfortunately, my chemo brain often buries the good ideas I create during meditation and recall is a BIG problem. As I established this week's affirmations, I realized what I previously taught for years: the value of association.

Voila: VHS = I am VITAL; I am HEALTHY; I am STRONG.

Thank you, Lord.

Notice that I'm affirming VHS as a *fait d'accompli*. That's my story and I'm sticking to it. And I came to that conclusion after my oncologist wouldn't give me chemo yesterday because of the number of still unhealed blisters in my mouth. It turns out that the new less-invasive chemo cocktail was more potent than my body could tolerate and the side effects (which lasted 11 days this time) turned me into a zombie.

On a positive note, my bilirubin is significantly down, which means the tumor in my lymph node has shrunk and is no longer pressing on my bile duct, and my liver enzymes are looking much better. Even so, next treatment next Wednesday. Keep those fingers and toes crossed.

I've taken some time during the last week to review journals I've written over the last 27 months. I am amazed at the number of unknowns, failures, and obstacles I've overcome. It even occurred to me that I could probably copy and paste so many of my journal entries from 2018, 2019, and even

2020, and no one would even know the difference. No wonder I'm so tired and so often frustrated beyond my capacity. But it is daily decision time: And I choose VHS.

Tomorrow is TGIF and I hope you have a fantastic weekend. I know we will: Scott and Liz are coming to Owen Lake Cottage for the first time since November and I can't wait to see them. Don't worry, they are taking the boat out first and we will maintain our social distance. Then we will take the boat out after they leave.

This spring in AR has been the most beautiful spring we have ever witnessed. We are in complete awe of the magnificence of Beaver Lake and the NWA foothills, greenery, and flowers: Fertilizer for the soul!

> With so much love and gratitude,
> K Sparky Strong

> "Karen, I love your VHS.
> My appt is Wednesday 9:00. I pray I will get to see you and we can visit.
> God has brought us together for a reason
> and I am so glad. I am praying for you to feel great
> while family is here and enjoy them.
> Love you, my new sweet sister."
> Kathy I

> "Wow, you are such a great friend to share your wisdom in good days and bad.
> Maybe you'll enjoy this, from Ishaan Tharoor, *Washington Post*:
> 'Amid its horrors and tragedies, the pandemic has driven home a startling reality.
> Travel bans and lockdowns have cleaned the globe, flushing the murk from
> Venice's canals, clearing Delhi's polluted smog, making distant snowy peaks
> visible for the first time in years from the shores of the Bosporus.
> With humans in retreat, nature has reclaimed what was once its own
> in whimsical ways: goats strutted through villages, antlered deer grazed
> on manicured city lawns, and mountain lions found perches by suburban fences.'
> What a vision. It inspired me to donate to the Climate Reality Project.
> Maybe others are finding more solace in nature and simple things.
> Hope is the bud of optimism. Missing you and remembering fondly our time
> together teaching with Cam, John, and Julie Lawson. XOX"
> Trudy McC

Bald for the 3rd Time
glad to have the laser machine back

"You make me laugh with your hair color story ordeal!!!
You are amazing!!! I'm praying you will get your chemo this week!!!
Hang in there :) XOXO"
Mary D

May 4, 2020

Monday, Monday - It's Monday morning and we did have a great weekend. We 'safely' took our neighbors out on our boat and then had dinner with Scott, Liz, and our much-missed Carson (5) and Amelia (3). Little Miss Amelia had a meltdown when she learned that she wasn't going to be able to spend the night in 'her' bed at Nana's house, but it made my heart sing that she still wants to be with Nana and Papa, even though we haven't seen her since Christmas. Thank goodness for FaceTime.

Oh, the joy of being grandparents.

Yesterday, Howard and I took a road trip to Eufalla, Oklahoma. Why in the world?

My brother Gary, who owns Phoenix Thera-lase, was driving from Dallas to bring me a laser therapy machine. He had lent me one of his laser therapy machines two years ago, and the results of laser therapy were amazing in these ways:

1) helping rebuild my immune system
2) reducing pain
3) treating my rheumatoid arthritis
4) reducing the swelling in my brain
5) rebuilding Howard's knee.

I am so grateful to Gary for this amazing gift. Now our laser therapy work begins. I'm probably the only person in the country with my very own laser machine and personal access to the man who knows more about the benefits of this therapy than anyone else. You can learn more about this game-changing therapy and all its applications on Gary's website: www. phoenixthera-lase.com. Thank you, Gary.

Three weeks ago, when I started my new chemo cocktail, Dr. Beck warned me that I might lose my hair again (my third time), and yesterday, as we were driving to OK, I looked down and was mortified to see clumps of hair falling on to my shirt. So today is shave my head day and I'm surprised at myself how emotional this is for me - again.

About a month ago I decided I really hated my new unruly gray, curly, wiry hair anyway. Though I dearly loved my Grandma Bellinger, every time I looked in the mirror, I saw her staring back at me with the hair I now have.

Being the person of action I am, I stopped at Walgreens and bought a box of hair color. Well, I had been warned: Chemo patients should not dye their hair because you never know what the chemicals will do to the color. Disregarding the warnings, I ended up with muddy grey hair with a pink sheen – worse than when I started.

Then, when I looked in the mirror, I saw my Nana Engel staring back at me. (Surely I'm not old enough to look like my grandmas.) I remember the pinkish cast to her white hair and I just couldn't stand it on my head. Back to the store for another box of color.

Alas, the outcome was the color of dirty sewer water. I looked worse than the images of both my grandmothers. It was so bad, Howard told me to shave my head. But since I still had illusions that I wouldn't lose all my hair again, I called my daughter-in-law, Liz, and asked her to contact her good friend Lana, a hair stylist.

Everyone agreed I had fried my hair and had few options for recovery. Lana sent some professional color to me at home and I colored my hair for the third time in three weeks. She also told me this was an interim color solution, because I need to wait three more weeks before she could help me move toward a color I can live with.

But, oh, have I learned my lesson. Alas, it doesn't matter: the shaver awaits.

As you can imagine, living with me and all my emotions, challenges, and chaos is a daily load for Howard. He has transference in his knee. When I'm feeling bad, his knees become more painful, and when I'm feeling better, his knees are less painful. And his dreams (or nightmares) reflect the stresses of his subconscious mind.

Howard decided to take action to ensure I would continue to fight my best fight. Howard knows I can't stand to waste money; it's just not in my German DNA. We always lease my cars because I do love new cars. I love my current car and told Howard I was glad we have 18 months to go on my current lease, because this would probably be my last lease.

Howard called the dealership and negotiated a 42-month lease on a beautiful new car, one I had loved when I saw it last fall. I walked into his office last week, he turned to me, smiled, and said, "I just bought you a new car."

"Sure, you're kidding."

And he smiled even bigger. "No, really, we'll pick it up when we go back to Austin at the end of May. You are so tight, you wouldn't die on me if you knew I'd still have to pay those lease payments, so you now need to live 42 months to fulfill the terms of the new lease, and I want you to think of me every time you get into your beautiful new car."

I've lived with this man almost 50 years, and this one of his most creative and compelling acts of love, based on Howard logic and practicality. SOOO Howard!

I'll love you forever, HHO.

Gearing up for the week, and hoping I'll be able to get my chemo Wednesday. Powering on!

Have a great week!

> With love and gratitude,
> K Sparky Strong

> "Thinking of you, Karen. xoxo...
> Are you going to leave us hanging?
> What kind of car did sweet Howard lease for you?
> Wishing you all the best."
> Barbara N

> "You always look beautiful! Go bald and beautiful!!!!
> What a sweet story about Howard. He is amazing,
> and I haven't even met him. Tell him he is being held high in my hand!!
> I'm so glad you got to be with some grandbabies.
> So good for the soul. Keep going, Karen Strong!!!
> You continue to teach us so many things.
> God loves your amazing heart and strength! XO"
> Denise H

THERE'S NO PLACE LIKE HOME
after 4.5 months in AR quarantine

"Surrounded by those you love is truly the best medicine.
Love, positive thoughts, and prayers continue to come your way.
Warmest regards from your 'Chicago' cousins!"
Gigi and Joe R

May 19, 2020

Home Sweet Home!

Who would have ever imagined that when we left at the beginning of December, we would not be back until mid-May? After being at Owen Lake Cottage since we came back from Camp Owen Colorado after Christmas, I had somewhat forgotten how special this home is to me: family photos, art from our world travels, a luxurious patio/pool area, and so may little 'things' that make any house a home. Loving every minute of being here!

Many of you have texted me to check on me after I haven't written in about two weeks. Do you know how wonderful, supported, and loved that makes me feel? And when we pulled in Thursday night, there was a beautiful floral arrangement on the front porch from my Bible Study Group. How special is that?

It has been a whirlwind since we came back.

Last Wednesday, I had chemo in AR; we drove back to Austin all day Thursday, unpacked Friday, and Steven, Shannon, and the kids brought Mexican food and stayed for a swim Friday night.

Saturday, my brother Gary and his girlfriend Debra brought me a laser machine (yay!) from Dallas and spent the night with us. Sunday, we went to Jeff and Lisa's ranch for lunch and to spend some time our grandkids. (ALL the grandkids have grown so much!) Laney and Riley cooked and baked from scratch, and let me tell you, their food was GREAT!

When we came home Sunday evening, my side effects started kicking in and I've spent the last 48 hours in chemo h@#$. No matter how much I expect it or consciously know it's coming, it is still hard to live through it.

But we're going to have a diversion tonight as Tiffany, Kyle, and the boys are bringing dinner.

How lucky am I to be able to see all my Austin children, their spouses, and grandchildren in the first few days of being home, especially since no one has seen anyone for months. Yes, we're staying outside, wearing masks, and social distancing while everyone swims, plays, and eats.

My spirit is rising because we are planning to see so many friends while we're home. My biggest challenge will be to moderate visits and ensure my safety. I'm planning to have my next three chemo treatments here in Austin, and am already scheduling dinners and morning coffee on the patio. So if you are in Austin and willing to social distance on my patio, I'd love to see you: please call me and let's get schedule our special time. In fact, it is supposed to be 100 degrees today, so be sure to bring your swimsuit and we will stay cool in the pool.

I certainly hope these side effects go away fast because I am NOT going to let them spoil my time in Austin. Full speed ahead (with naps every day!). Loving the heat and sun.

Additional note:

While I was at the AR Oncology Center last week, I met with Dr. Lambeada. I thought he was only the doctor who could approve my AR Medical marijuana card for my CBD with THC. Little did I know he is so much more. He is a specialist who addresses the 'whole' cancer and PTSD patient. He was soon sharing how he could help mitigate side effects, work through goals, quality of life issues, etc. etc. etc.

It was an amazing session, one I hope will evolve with time as we find out if this new chemo is successful. Stay tuned for CT scan results on June 24.

With love and gratitude,
K Sparky Strong

"You are so strong and such an inspiration.
I am thrilled you are home and reunited with family at this time.
Miss you much - you lit up the room at our training sessions.
Hugs. And prayers."
Amy C

An Absolutely Fabulous 71st Birthday
Steven and Shannon throw a drive-by birthday party

"You looked radiant on your birthday!!!
Hope you could feel all the love.
Am praying for you every day
and especially for good results on your CT scan this week.
No matter what, stay Karen Strong!!!
I admire your resilience and beautiful heart and spirit."
Donna H

June 11, 2020

Balloons, streamers, flowers, gifts, a gazillion cards. What an exciting way to celebrate my 71st birthday last week!

A great big THANK YOU to son STEVEN and daughter-in-law SHANNON for the best and most amazing drive-by car parade in the history of Austin. I sat under a shade tree and acted like queen for a day. I did say 71st birthday: now videoed for the annals of history. (video link - https://vimeo.com/434770736 - pw = Karen)

A big thank you to all who came and supported my big celebration. I will never forget your outpouring of love and support. (And of course, a big thank you to Mz P., *aka* Sandy Perkins, for her help and home-baked cookies passed out by my beautiful grandkids).

I do plan to write thank you notes, but this big task will take me quite awhile, so please grant me time, lots of it.

What else happened while I was home in Austin for a month after being quarantined in AR for almost five months?

First, I saw more friends during the 28 days I was there than I normally would have seen in six months during 'normal' times, all with masks, social distancing, and lots of soap. WHAT A HIGH! From coffees to lunches to happy hours to dinners: all very therapeutic, energizing and fun, fun, fun to be with family and so many friends.

At the same time, I had three straight weeks of chemo in Austin accompanied by the dreaded follow-on side effects. Then after the last infusion on my birthday a week ago, we brought granddaughters Laney and Riley back to AR for a whirlwind week of fun-in-the-sun water activities and exploration. I will admit, it was a challenge to do all the things I had planned for the girls during my week of complete exhaustion, digestive issues, and a mouth full of blisters. But I couldn't let all that interfere with my 1 week with my girls.

And Howard was the BEST Papa. When I just couldn't get out of bed, he took over and drove them out to Crystal Bridges, gave them architectural lessons on the homes we're building, took them knee-boarding and tubing on the boat, and then out to eat.

Now I'm focused on my upcoming CT scan on Wednesday. Big day to find out if the new chemo cocktail I've been on for the last 90 days has been effective. I'm going to be soooo irritated I've had to endure all that I have, if this chemo isn't effective.

And even more disconcerting, if not successful, what's next? Will let you know the results Friday. Prayers and fingers crossed until then!

> With love and gratitude,
> K Sparky Strong

"As I said in my card, seeing you all dressed up for the party
will be a highlight of my summer!!!
Thanks to you for one heck of a birthday celebration!!!"
Nancy McC

"So LOVED being with you!!! You did fit in quite a bit of FUN!!!
Way to go! Strong prayers and positive vibes for Friday!
It just HAS to be making a difference!! You look fabulous,
and you have had great energy in all your activities!
Sending lots of love!!"
Carol C

SHRINKING, SHRINKING, SHRUNK!
AND THE WINNER IS:
K SPARKY STRONG
closing the first phase
of my bumpy cancer journey

"I've got a smile from ear-to-ear :-)
I knew that if anyone could do it, it would be you.
Wow! Way to go, partner."
Cam S

June 24, 2020

Gloria… G-l-o-r-i-a. Thank you to the Lord Almighty from whom all good things flow.

Such astonishing news revealed on today's CT scan. Though pancreatic cancer does not go into 'remission' as we think of it, Dr. Beck was delighted to announce I'm in remission just a few hours ago (after my CT scan today); he was chuckling and smiling from ear to ear. He was almost as happy as Howard and I are.

The tumors in my lungs and on my bile duct have all shrunk. And, even more of a miracle, my original pancreatic and liver tumors look like inactive scar tissue. WOW! Unreal.

Though I would love a 'maintenance' pill to prevent tumor regrowth, there currently isn't one for pancreatic cancer patients like me. The goal for the next 90 days is for the tumors NOT to regrow as they did before, so I will be doing chemo every other week, and we'll reassess the situation in September.

The one bad note is my low, low, low potassium level; so I'm taking lots of pills and having IV infusions a couple times a week. Dr. Beck said he would be following my blood work every two weeks when I come in for my chemo but he didn't need to see me until my next CT in September.

How's that for 'good results'?

I did it! My promise to Howard was that I would make it to our 50th wedding anniversary on August 29th. Then we decided to have a small casual party weekend up here at Owen Lake Cottage for our families (extended, and there are a lot of us) and include a few long-term, best friends who are like family to us. Now I'm going to start planning. Karen and Howard's 50th anniversary will now be a reality. Time for me to get to work!

This is almost the end of Phase 1 of my Cancer Journey. I have documented so many ways this 'attack' on me has allowed me to grow and change. As I often say in my meditations: "Thank you, cancer, for helping me realize what's important in life. Thank you for helping me learn and live a more meaningful life in God/Jesus Christ. I've learned, and now it is time for you to go."

One of the most in-my-face lessons is that we have have complex self-healing powers yet unexplored and under-utilized in traditional western medicine. If you go back to the beginning of my journey, you will see how many out-of-the-box approaches and methodologies I've tried to incorporate in my quest for continued life (remember how I earned the name 'Sparky'?).

But first and foremost, I believe God does have a plan for each of us, we really don't have control over our destiny, family/friends' support coupled with the power of prayer is #1 above all.

I could go on and on, but that's why you are reading this book. My greatest ambition is for you to live the hard-learned legacy of 'K Sparky Strong'. Make it your own.

Since I am now in maintenance doing chemo bi-weekly for the next 90 days, you won't hear from me unless there is some new wrinkle (like an immunotherapy for pancreatic patients trial). Because I don't know how long this chemo will work until my body rejects it (and it will at some point), I'm praying for imminent cures and trials. Howard is still depending on that 42-month car lease to keep me motivated.

Today, it seems highly doable. Sure I'll still have those god-awful side effects, but knowing the cancer is 'in remission' makes the rest of it easier to tolerate.

Please continue to keep me in your thoughts and prayers. You have become like family over the last 2½ years, and I certainly don't want to lose touch. I am just completing Phase 1 of this journey, and you will hear from me starting again in September. Have a wonderful summer - stay safe and cool!

Don't hesitate to reach out to me any time. I will continue to pray for your family's health, safety, and happiness.

> With so much love and gratitude,
> K Sparky Strong

"WOW!!!!! FABULOUS!!!!!!!!
You ARE incredible!!! 50th Anniversary, here you come!
It will be such a beautiful special celebration!!
And... yep... 42 months, and a renewal?
lots of love and many hugs to you!!!"
Carol C

"Oh my... tears of joy to witness a true divine miracle!
Thank you, dear Lord, for this amazing gift of hope and healing!
We love you, Karen, and the prayers will not stop!"
Penny G

"Whoohooo!!!! What amazing news.
I am so thrilled!
You just turned my whole day around
and reminded me of what's important!"
Sara VS

"Karen, I have goosebumps!
I can't tell you how excited I am for you.
What an inspiration you are to everyone who has had cancer.
Praying for you daily and may God bless you and keep you
through this very difficult journey. xoxo"
Ree O'C

IN CLOSING

2020 has been a tough year for almost everyone on the planet – and for me, it has been a daily battle to stay alive and functional. Yet even so, I can measure the frequent steps toward weakness and further lack of abilities and independence.

That said, I'm still not ready to give up. I promised Howard and the kids I would keep trying for as long as I can – so here I am.

Step by step – day by day! One day at a time. My journey continues.

The last three years have been life changing, and my spiritual journey has been challenging, touching – yet emotionally charged and so over-whelming. I cannot even fathom the number of prayer warriors who have continued to pray for me for three years now. How can that be?

This book is for you and I hope, as a result, you will gain an under-standing of the concepts of:

1) taking it one day at a time.

2) trusting in the Lord and patience and being open to accepting His plan for you,

3) knowing He loves you and will always be with you – regardless.

The challenge is I'd like to know what that plan is. It's that control that is hard to relinquish after decades of trying steer the Owen ship across choppy waves to safe haven.

I will continue to respond to the name my late friend Judy gave me: 'K Sparky Strong'. I've earned the name and will keep working to support others and share some of the hard-learned lessons I have uncovered over the last 3 years. (Judy, I will continue to make you proud.)

I hope this book speaks for itself and that you, too, will benefit from all the lessons I have worked so hard to incorporate in my life. This is my gift to you.

"For I know the plans I have for you, declares the Lord, "plans to prosper you and not to harm you, plan to give you a hope and a future."

Jeremiah 29:11

"God has not promised skies always blue, flower-strewn pathways all our lives through; God has not promised sun without rain, joy without sorrow, peace without pain.

But God has promised strength for the day, rest for the labor, light for the way, grace for the trials, help from above, unfailing sympathy, undying love."

Addie Johnson Flint

"No eye has seen, nor ear heard, nor the heart of man imagined, what GOD HAS PREPARED FOR THOSE WHO LOVE HIM."

1 Corinthians 2:9

Acknowledgments

Because this book is for all of you, I'd like to list the people who made my journey so much better. I could not have done everything I did without the love, encouragement, support, prayers, and heartfelt messages, phone calls, text, and emails. You are truly my "wall of angels."

Alegria H	Diane & Jerry	Kathy R
Amy C	Donna H	Katy C
Anna S	Elaine H	Kay K
Auddie W	Elizabeth O	Kendyl R
Barbara N	Elizabeth T	Kim H
Barbara B	Fran B	Laurie B
Beatriz F	Gail R	Lavon M
Becky H	Gigi & Joe R	Leah L
Becky R	Geri P	Leigh H
Belinda K	Glen B	Lisa K
Betsy & Mark	Greg S	Liz O
Bonnie D	Jacquetta F	Lori P
Bonnie F	Jan S	Lynn N
Cameron S	Jane B	Lynn T
Carl McI	Janet M	Maggie H
Carol S	Janie C	Margi F
Cathy E	Jeani & Col. John S	Mari L
Cathy P	Jeanne C	Marianne C
Cindy H	Jeanne S	Marion M
Cindy J	Jenny B Q	Mark K
Cindy W	Jerry D	Mark O
Colleen L	Jill T	Martha C
Cookie B	John D	Martha V
Courtney R	Jo Lynne B	Marlene H
Deb Davis G	Judy W	Mary C
Deb W	Julie M	Mary D
Debbi B	Kat B	Mary Ann G
Debbie C	Kathleen B	Mary Gay G
Debbie S	Kathy G	Mark O
Denise H	Kathy P	Melisa B
Diane H	Kathy & Richard	Mike H

Missy H
Mollie C
Nancy McC
Nannette O
Pam W
Pansy F
Patricia N
Patti H
Patty B
Peggy H
Penny G
Penny P
Rachel K
Raghbir K
Ree O'C
Rose Betty W
Rosemary L
Sadi K
Sandy P
Sara V S
Scott W
Sharon W
Susan R
Susan W
Susie D
Suzanne M
Terry T
Trudy McC

Karen Bellinger Owen

June 11, 1949 ~ January 15, 2021

"My sheep listen to my voice; I know them, and they follow me.
I give them eternal life, and they shall never perish."

JOHN 10:27-28

Private Memorial

Owen Residence, Austin, Texas
January 23, 2021
Eleven o'clock in the morning

Prelude

Jonathan Moody, guitar

Duet

"Sissy's Song"
Liz Owen and Jonathan

Welcome

Howard Owen
Margaret Collis

Solo

"Wildflowers"
Jonathan

Reflections

Tiffany Miller
Jeffrey Owen

Solo

"Go Rest High Upon the Mountain"
Jonathan

Reflections

Steven Owen
Scott Owen
Howard Owen

Closing

∽

Luncheon to follow

Karen Bellinger Owen

Karen (Bellinger) Owen was born on June 11, 1949 to loving parents John and Patricia Bellinger of Chicago, Illinois and peacefully passed away, welcomed home to the Lord, on January 15, 2021. She fought a most admirable and courageous fight against Stage 4 Pancreatic cancer, a grim diagnosis she was given three years ago for which she was assigned just three weeks to live. She tackled this challenge head on, with great determination, as she did with everything else in her life. She immediately began researching, reading everything she and her son Steven could get their hands on, seeking out the most experienced doctors, exploring the most up to date options and trials. She even adopted less conventional treatments (dog dewormer, singing bowls, dissonant piano playing, etc.) and left absolutely no stone unturned. And she did all of this under the cloud of the tragic death of her beloved son, Blake, who passed away just four months before her diagnosis. Dealing with that gut wrenching trauma and moving quickly to fight her disease took more courage and physical stamina than most can muster in a lifetime.

Karen's efforts were rewarded with three challenging yet wonderful years, as she refused to allow the disease to rob her of living her life. She joyfully celebrated her 50th wedding anniversary with the love of her life, Howard, the births of two more grandchildren, holidays with the family at Camp Owen Colorado and Camp Owen Ozarks, more than 50 birthdays of all her 5 children and 12 grandchildren, and hosted a Valentine's Day tea for 125 of her friends to name just a few. And she did it with the gut and grace – and humor – that all who knew her to be true.

Between these events, Karen managed to write a 300-page memoir of her 35-month cancer journey, *Three Weeks to Live*, so others with cancer and their families can learn from her experience. That was Karen – always thinking of others and how she could make a positive difference in their lives. She also maintained a CaringBridge account throughout her ordeal, updating her friends and family with uplifting and oftentimes humorous accounts of her experience. Aptly signed each time "Karen Sparky Strong." And "Strong" was an understatement of who she was.

Karen graduated tenth in her class from Regina Dominican High School in Wilmette, IL. She was the first in her family to graduate college (University of Missouri - Columbia). She continued her education by graduating from Harvard Graduate School of Business' OPM Program. After cofounding and serving as the COO of Builder's Update, she supervised its sale to a subsidiary of Kohlberg, Kravis, and Roberts of NYC. At the age of 50, she joined an IBM subsidiary as a National Facilities Manager, eventually rising to the role of IBM's Director of Education Worldwide Software, traveling to 65 countries on four continents.

Karen was also the president of the Women's Symphony League of Austin and Austin Dance

Club, and also a member of the Junior Austin Woman's Club, Austin Woman's Club, The Assembly, Art Guild of Laguna Gloria, and Austin Natural Science Association Guild. She also had many special friends in her Lunch Bunch, Bible Study Group and Book Club. She was a loyal and devoted friend to all and took great pride in her relationships.

While Karen's investments of time and energy into business and professional endeavors proved successful and fulfilling, her true feelings of success came from raising her five children. She felt immense pride and celebrated each of their accomplishments, and will be forever missed by Jeff and wife Lisa (Laney, Riley, and Ford), Steven and wife Shannon (Westyn, Liam, Brazos, and Aspen), Scott and wife Elizabeth (Carson and Amelia), and Tiffany and husband Kyle (Ethan and Kalen). Karen is survived by her sisters Jeanne Sogge and Mary Ann Chapman, brothers Glen Bellinger and Gary Bellinger, and numerous nieces and nephews. Karen is predeceased by her granddaughter Averie Isabella Owen and her youngest, cherished son, Blake Andrew Owen. Not far behind the unconditional devotion to her children and grandchildren was the unwavering love she had for her lifelong partner and husband Howard. He proposed to her only two weeks after meeting her as a Freshman at the University of Illinois and after an all too long 36-month courtship (Karen played her hard-to-get game), they married and moved to Austin in 1972 from Chicago creating a life of community and never looked back. Their marriage was magical; one of passion, respect, encouraging individual successes, and not going to bed angry. (Howard did most of the apologizing.) Their role modeling set a strong example for their own children to select partners for long, enduring marriages.

Only with the loving, creative, and dedicated care of Joseph Beck, M.D., and Debra Tooker, APNR, of Highlands Oncology Group of NW Arkansas, her brother Gary's Phoenix Laser Systems, and the ever insightful guidance of Elyse Rosen, LCSW, could Karen have stretched three weeks to three years. Her family is forever grateful for their knowledge, tenacity, and care.

To see her life in photos, click on https://karensparkystrong.com.

A celebration of Karen's life will be held in the future based on Covid recommendations.

The family requests that in lieu of flowers, donations may be made to the Grace Grego Maxwell Dell Children's Mental Health Unit (4900 Mueller Boulevard, Austin, Texas 78723) in memory of Blake Owen or the Central Texas Food Bank (6500 Metropolis Drive, Austin, Texas 78744), causes very close to Karen's heart.

It is difficult to put into words Karen's remarkable life and the many people she impacted along her way. Her legacy will live on far beyond her years on earth. May her memory be an eternal blessing to all who knew and loved Karen.

Made in the USA
Coppell, TX
27 August 2022

82172146R00155